NEPAL: TRANSITION TO DEMOCRATIC REPUBLICAN STATE

Nepal

Transition To Democratic Republican State

(2008 Constituent Assembly)

B.C. Upreti

KALPAZ

Nepal: Transition to Democratic Republican State

Rs. 690

ISBN: 978-81-7835-774-4

Published in 2010 in India by
Kalpaz Publications
C-30, Satyawati Nagar, Delhi-110052
E-mail: kalpaz@hotmail.com
Laser Typesetting at: Tact Computer Graphics, Delhi
Printed at: Young Art Press, Delhi-110092

Contents

Preface

Nepal's journey from a constitutional monarchy to a republican state has been full of ups and downs. It was way back in 1950 that Nepal stepped on the path of constitutionalism and democracy. At that time also demand for a Constituent Assembly was raised by the Communist Party of Nepal. It was never accepted so long as the monarchy remained a powerful political institution.

The Maoists for the first time challenged the monarchic state of Nepal in an organized way through an insurgency in 1996. They pleaded for a republican state and a new constitution for the country prepared by people's representatives. The elections to the Constitution Assembly in April 2008 have been a significant landmark in the contemporary Nepalese politics. It is indeed a significant step towards consolidation of peace process in the country. The elections of the Constituent Assembly are significant also in the context that it has set a tone for the direction of the Nepalese politics. Nepal has already been declared a republic and the Communist Party of Nepal (Maoist) has formed a coalition government under the leadership of Pushpa Kamal Dahal "Prachanda".

The Constituent Assembly has exhibited an inclusive character and that way it is a significant development. But there are a large number of other issues like federalism, management of Maoist combatants, challenges of socio-economic reconstruction and above all the framing of a new constitution. The new government has to face all these challenges.

The present study is focused upon the Constituent Assembly elections and its after meth. Most of the data on the CA elections has been taken from the website of Nepal Election Commission and the related sites.

I would like to take this opportunity to express my sincere thanks to my colleagues, friends, research scholars and students who have encouraged me to undertake this study. My family members: Savita, Neha & Navendva have always stood by my side in my academic ventures, so my deep gratitude's to them.

A word of appreciation for Shri Mahendra Singh not only for computer typing but also helping me in procuring the data on elections.

The Nepalese political scenario is fastly changing. Therefore, such a study has its limitations. I am aware of it but still hope that it would be greatly helpful to the scholars and students of Nepalese politics in updating their knowledge of the contemporary Nepali politics.

Jaipur **B.C. Upreti**
9 September 2008

1

Democracy and Constitutionalism in Nepal

Nepal's history of democracy and constitutionalism almost coincided with the withdrawal of the colonial rule form South Asia and the down of democracy in India, Pakistan and Sri Lanka. It was towards the last phase of the Rana rule that the need for a constitution was felt in order to contain the rising popular discontent against the authoritarian rule of the Ranas. But neither could the efforts of the Rana Prime Minister to introduce a constitution in the country succeed nor could the Rana political system be saved against the forces of change. Resultantly, Nepal steped on the path of constitutionalism and democracy. However, Nepal had a fragile history of constitutionalism and democracy. The Nepalese rulers neither could provide a broad based constitution nor laid down a strong foundation of democratic institutions in the country. Despite Nepal's way to a democratic political order, the traditional authoritarian power elite represented by monarchy, remained at the centre stage of politics.[1] The authoritarian rulers had a vested interest in making the democratic institutions weak and fragile. The democratic elite looked towards the institution of monarchy for its survival and sustenance. As a result despite establishment of a democratic system after the 1990 movement the democratic governments failed in initiating any structural changes except the creation of political super structures, so as to meet the constitutional requirements of the democratic governance.

The Maoist insurgency, which Nepal had faced for a decade has once again brought the country to a critical phase of political and constitutional change. In order to understand the dynamics of the upcoming constitutional and political transformation in Nepal, it is desirable to make an assessment of the main currents of constitutional and democratic changes in Nepal since 1950.

NATURE AND DIRECTION OF POLITICAL CHANGE IN NEPAL

Nepal had been ruled for centuries within an authoritarian political set up first by the Shah Monarchs and later by the Rana Prime Minister for more than hundred years. Both the Shaha and the Rana rulers believed in a highly centralized, personalized and absolutist political order. The state remained synonymous to the authoritarian rule and people were treated as state subjects in an absolutist manner. The Shah rulers also tried to use the emotional feelings of the masses by using religio - cultural sentiments in imposing itself as a representative of god on earth. It helped consolidation of the monarchic rule politically as well as socio, culturally. The Shah rulers tried to create a monolithic socio – cultural order in Nepal within the fold of Hinduism at the top of which was the Hindu monarch. The monarchy not only became the repository of the state but also the socio – cultural order of the country. The non – Hindu communities had no option but to accept the Hinduised social structure and the monarchic state. There was no room for any dissent.

The Rana rulers not only accepted but further consolidated the existing socio – cultural order of the country. The Rana rulers however did not enjoy the kind of religio – cultural foundation that the Shah rulers had. They followed a policy of patronization and punishment. The Ranas did not allow any kind of dissent within the society. The Rana rule had survived on tyranny, revenge and persecution.[2]

But they could not prevent dissent brewing against them out side Nepal. The Nepalese living in India and inspired by the Indian social reforms and the Nationalist Movement started organizing themselves to voice against the atrocities of the Rana rulers. It was since nineteen thirties that such organized efforts were being made. Some of them also went to Nepal to launch protest movements against the Ranas but they were treated much harshly by the Ranas. So the possibilities of launching any kind of protest movement from within Nepal were thwarted. The formation of the Nepali Congress and the Communist Party of Nepal towards the end of the decade of the forties was a clear indication of the increasing organizational strength of the Nepalese living in India and their determination to fight against the authoritarian rule of the Ranas. It is needless to point out here that these Nepalese were influenced by the Indian social reform movement and the movement against the British colonial rule. The Indian National Movement itself provided an opportunity of political apprenticeship to a large number of Nepalese who had been members of the Indian National Congress and took part in its activities. The Indian political leaders provided them ideological and political support. The easy accessibility to India due to the open border with Nepal, educational facilities, etc. were the other supportive factors.

The Rana rulers had tried to maintain friendly relations with the British government in India, so as to seek support from them to their rule.[3] But it was not possible to check the growth of anti – Rana activities taking place in India. Varanasi and Calcutta were the main centres of activitie of the Nepalese living in India. It seems that in the over all context the Indian National Movement provided an umbrella to the growing anti – Rana sentiments among the Nepalese living in India.[4]

The Nepali Congress decided to launch an armed struggle against the Ranas from the Tarai region in 1950. But before its movement could take any shape the Rana rule came to an end in a dramatic way. It is true that the Nepali Congress was preparing for an arms struggle but the fact remains that the Rana rule was not overthrown through a mass movement. Consequently the Nepali Congress and the other democratic forces of Nepal were not the sole deciding factor about the future of democracy in Nepal.

In the tripartite agreement held in New Delhi in 1951 between the King, Ranas and the Nepali Congress it was decided to follow a middle way approach regarding the future of democracy in the country.

It seems that three factors had been significant in bringing the 1950 revolution to an end. Firstly, the dramatic escape of king Tribhuwan from the royal palace to the Indian Embassy at Kathmandu. The king was perhaps foreseeing restoration of his powers. As soon as the king reached New Delhi it was decided to withdraw the movement. Thus, before the movement could take roots in the kingdom it came to a sudden end. Secondly, in the New Delhi Agreement of 1951, India, because of the treaty that it had concluded with the Rana rulers, and also because of her own strategic interests in the Himalayan region, did not favour total uprooting of the traditional order. She in fact believed that it might create political chaos, which would not be in the interest of either Nepal or India. There was also perhaps an understanding that Nepal did not have sufficient internal conditionalities to support the installation of democracy. It was therefore thought of moving towards democracy in a gradual manner. Nehru termed it as a middle way approach. His middle way approach might be justified in the then prevailing conditions, but not from the point of view of the growth of democracy in the kingdom in the long run. In fact, the net result was that the 1950 movement was reduced to a mere restoration of powers of the monarchy. It did not help much in the strengthening of democracy in the country in the following years.

The Indian Memorandum of 8 December 1950, as well as February 1951 New Delhi Agreement had emphasized the formation of a Constituent Assembly in order to prepare a new constitution for Nepal.[5] But it was never materialized. Even in 1959 when the new constitution of Nepal came into force, king Mahendra did not accept demand for the formation of a Constituent Assembly and he himself constituted a committee to prepare a constitution. Thus a basic provision regarding the promulgation of the constitution through a duly elected Constituent Assembly could not be made effective. It appears that the monarchy had a vested interest in not conceding to the demand for a Constituent Assembly. It shows that the traditional elite was still assertive; that it was not subscribed to democratic norms and beliefs; that it was interested in the democratization of the polity only to the extent, which was essential in order to fulfill certain commitments on their part. It soon became clear that the democratic forces were dominated by the traditional elite.

The political parties which played a major role in the overthrow of the Rana regime and which were expected to function for the stabilization of the democratic system failed in taking the Nepalese political system to an appropriate direction. On the contrary, the manner in which the party politics went on, it only paved a way for the emergence of the royal authority. It also gave an opportunity to the monarchy to label the activities of the political parties undemocratic and unfavourable to the prevailing conditions of Nepal. In fact, the Nepalese politics in the post 1951 period was marked by the emergence of a large number of political parties and groups on the one hand and continuous fragmentation, group politics and personal rivalries among them on the other. Due to the endless rivalry and scramble for power among major political parties and politicians and the conflict of leadership the goal of democracy was lost. The people were alienated. In fact, the political parties failed in providing leadership to the masses. In their quest for acquiring political power they had indeed, undermined the necessity of creating adequate socio-economic conditions for the sustenance of democracy in the kingdom. It seems that the political parties lacked experience, a sound mass base and a clear programme.

The political situation in the country in fact, ensured re-emergence of traditional elite under the leadership of monarchy. The old land-owing class and the Rana families found sufficient opportunity to promote their personal interests. It was obvious that they had a common interest in defeating the reform measures of the Nepali Congress.[6] The people were not much concerned to the emerging political patterns, since the basic socio-economic structure had remained unchanged, for which they were rather more concerned. They indeed lacked political consciousness and mobilization. Army and the bureaucracy also represented interests of the traditional forces. It was very difficult to challenge their interests. The press, which is considered to be a source of interest articulation and interest aggregation in an emerging society remained largely devoid of this role particularly due to its primitive stage of growth. It may again be stressed here that the country lacked a feasible socio-economic infrastructure base for the working of democracy.

It should also be pointed out here that the nationalism, which took roots in Nepal towards the middle of the fifties had a narrow basis. In fact, the traditional elite in its quest for reassertion of political power, found India's special relationship with Nepal a major obstacle. Hence, it raised the bogey of anti-Indianism. It soon became a major tool of assertive nationalism and the political elite of Nepal failed in developing a broad-based nationalism, which would have been supportive of democracy. Thus the Nepali society lacked those basic premises that were essential for the growth of democracy.

As pointed out earlier, Nepal lacked an appropriate socio – economic background for the working of democracy and little efforts were made in that direction. The Rana rulers had deliberately kept the country backward as it suited to their interest. In 1951 when Rana rule came to an end Nepal did not have even the basic economic infrastructure. There were no means of transportation and communication, no industries and no basic amenities for the masses.

Installation and Abrogation of Democracy

In 1959 Nepal was endowed with a democratic constitution and parliamentary government after the 1959 general elections. The Nepali Congress got an absolute majority and formed the government under the leadership of B.P. Koirala. But this system could not work for long. In December 1960, King Mahendra abrogated the parliament and took powers in his hands. In fact, King Mahendra had expressed, more than once, his dissatisfaction over the functioning of the Koirala government. King Mahendra's own justification of the steps taken by him was that it was done in order to save the people and the country. A few days before the royal takeover he said in a speech that : "the fair name of democracy should never be permitted to be exploited, to do evil rather than good to the people.[7] He had further made it clear the he too had certain responsibilities and he would not hesitate in taking steps in order to fulfill those responsibilities.[8] He alleged the Koirala Ministry for its failure in improving law and order situation in the country. He said that situation had compelled him to take steps in the interest of the people. However, it was not convincing that his concern for the deteriorating conditions of the country alone had led him to abrogate the parliamentary system. In fact, what appears to be more logical is that he had distaste for the western style of democracy and did not want to see it taking roots in the country. He had expressed his disliking for the parliamentary democracy as early as 1955. In a speech on 8th May 1955, he said "...... four round years have passed since democracy was brought in by the joint efforts of us all. During this period the government has been run by several cabinets of ministers.... The balance sheet of profit and loss to the people from these various experiments is before the people......... concrete achievements could not be ensured from such a state of affairs".[9] In spite of his personal disliking for the western democratic system, King Mahendra in order to keep the promise of his late father, agreed for a new constitution and holding parliamentary elections in 1959. King Mahendra had to accept people's verdict for the time being. But his ambitions and lust for power ultimately compelled him to take a drastic step, such as, the abrogation of the infant parliamentary democracy. He was clear in his perception that if democracy would come to stay in Nepal he would not be able to assert in politics. It is clear that he believed that if the parliamentary system would be stabilized in Nepal he would remain a figure head for ever, without any powers. He was not prepared to compromise with such a situation.

Nepal's Experiment with Third World Model of Democracy

King Mahendra moved towards searching an alternative political order, which would establish supremacy of the monarchy and at the same time, fulfill minimum democratic aspirations of the people of Nepal. With this objective he appointed a 'Constitution Committee' to study the political systems of some of the developing countries, like Pakistan, Indonesia, Egypt, Nigeria and Yugoslavia. These were the countries that had established political system claimed to be as the 'third world model of democracy'. It is interesting to note here that in these countries the so-called alternative democratic political order was evolved by the authoritarian rulers in order to legitimize their own authorities, such as, Ayub Khan in Pakistan, Sukarno in Indonesia and Nasser in Egypt.[10]

The underlined assumptions behind studying the politico-administrative institutions of these countries were stated to be that; (i) the western democracies had failed in the third world societies, therefore, such a political order was needed which would be based on the "cultural tradition and wisdom of the people of the third world countries', (ii) it was not possible to establish democracy by imposing it on people from above. It should operate at the 'grass root' level and develop upward, (iii) in underdeveloped societies the political parties were obstacles in the evolution and development of the democratic institutions. Therefore, the political system should function without any formal political organizations.

The Constitution Committee suggested for the establishment of 'Panchayat System', which obviously resembled Ayub's 'Basic Democracy', Sukarno's 'Guided Democracy' and the 'Class Organization' System of Egypt and Nigeria. The main features of the panchayat system were; "party less" character of the polity, supremacy of the monarchy and its guidance and control at all levels of the panchayat organizations; decentralization of political power and class coordination. King Mahendra described the new political order as a truly 'Nepali' political system based on the culture and tradition of Nepal. Hence, it was considered as an 'indigenous political order.[11]

The panchayat system provided for a four-tier hierarchical organization with the National Panchayat at the top followed by zonal, district and village or town panchayats in the descending order. The representatives to the village or town panchayats, which formed lowest tier of the panchayat system, were elected directly by the village or town assemblies constituted by the adult population of the villages or towns within its boundaries. Above to village or town panchayats the indirect method of election was in practice wherein the representatives of the lower tier elected representatives to the higher tiers of the panchayats.[12] 1962 panchayat constitution also provided for a council of ministers headed by a Prime Minister appointed by the king. The council of ministers was an administrative body responsible for the implementation of the policies and programmes of His Majesty. The king was at the top of the system holding all the powers of a sovereign ruler. Every organization within the system was under his guidance and control. He was the repository of all legislative, executive and judicial powers. Apart from this, there were certain institutions that were formed with the objective of popularizing the panchayat ideology in the countryside, and creating support for the panchayat system under the active leadership of the king. Thus, a guidance council was formed to coordinate the activities of various class organizations. In 1967, 'Back to the Village National Campaign' (BVNC) was launched as an ideological move with a view to popularizing 'Panchayat Philosophy' in the countryside.[13]

The democratic organizations though banned under the new system did not accept it and decided to launch a struggle for the restoration of the parliamentary democracy in the country. The panchayat system obviously could not gain popularity among the different sections of the society and the democratic forces remained a potent threat to the panchayat system in the following years. They initially demanded liberalization of the panchayat system. Later on, such demands were also being raised from within the panchayat system. It shows that there was over centralization of powers and the popular demands were not taken into consideration. It gave rise to dissatisfaction among the masses, especially, the students, who were annoyed with the policies of the government. The discontent of the people further grew as the government tried to consolidate the powers of monarchy instead of broadening the system and taking the people into confidence. It, however, ultimately brought the system at a turning point towards, the early months of 1979, when demands were raised for the abolition of the of the panchayat system. It reflects that a large section of the people had lost confidence over the panchayat system.

It appears that the partyless character of the panchayat system was a personal liking of king Mahendra. He was of the opinion that the political parties could function only in a developed society. But actually they were not allowed to function as they were considered a threat to the position of the king. But due to non existence of political parties the panchayat system was faced with a serious lacuna. While it aimed at establishing democracy at the "grass root" level, it did not have any mechanism to provide political education to the poor, illiterate and traditional people. Though, motives behind the formation of class organizations were to use them as a substitute to the political parties, they were not allowed to participate in organized political activities. It is a moot question whether any organization could fulfill political functions without having certain basic political rights. However, despite ban on the political parties their activities could not be stopped and they indeed posed a perpetual threat to the panchayat system from both within and outside government.

The structures and powers of the panchayats were not in conformity with the responsibilities assigned to them. The National Panchayat, which was the highest legislative body of the country, did not have a truly representative character. Its members were indirectly elected. The powers and functions of the National Panchayat were limited to discussions on various issues and to make recommendations. On certain cases, like royal family, National Panchayat had to take prior permission for a discussion on them in the house. The decentralization of powers in the panchayat hierarchies was missing in practice. At the levels of district and village or town panchayats there were parallel hierarchies of government officials, panchayat workers and the Back to the village National campaign officials. The panchayats remained subservient to other more powerful parallel institutions.

The panchayat system failed in bringing any change in the traditional patterns of power. The upper caste domination continued in the panchayat organizations as well. The lower caste groups, Tribals and Madhes his remained isolated from the politico-administrative structures.

The panchayat system also remained non-responsive to the popular aspirations and demands. On the contrary, attempts were made by both king Mahendra and king Birendra to consolidate their position.[14] The economy of the country could not make any significant advance particularly towards meeting basic needs of the people.

The failure of the panchayat system in broadening itself and meeting basic needs of the people gradually led it towards a crisis. Interestingly at a time when the dissatisfaction was gradually brewing among various sections of the Nepalese society, the return of Nepali Congress leaders, B.P. Koirala and Ganesh Man Singh, to Nepal in December 1976, after a long exile in India, was highly encouraging to the democratic forces. It gave a new hope and strength to those who had been constantly demanding for the liberalization of the panchayat system.[15] Soon after his return to Kathmandu, B.P. Koirala called for a national reconciliation with the king in favour of the parliamentary system. He also called for a mass movement for the reestablishment of democracy in the country. It was since then that panchayat system was drawn into a crisis and ultimately to a serious jolt during 1979 mass movement. king Birendra declared to hold a referendum in May, 1980 in order to defuse the crisis.[16]

Much hopes were pinned on the May 1980 referendum, which the country was to hold in order to decide whether to continue with the panchayat system or a change over to the multi-partly system. The Nepali Congress and other parties of the kingdom were much hopeful about results of the referendum. The Nepali Congress indeed was over enthusiastic about its performance and thought that it alone would be able to form the government independently after the result of referendum goes in favour of the multi-partly system. However, to a great dismay of the political parties, the result of the referendum went in favour of the continuation of the panchayat system. Thus, the possibility to abandon the panchayat system through constitutional means got frustrated. The panchayat system was reformed in December 1980 through an amendment to the 1962 constitution.

The attitude of the political parties towards the subsequent constitutional reforms, which provided for direct elections to the National Panchayat, was obviously not fabourable. Their main objection was that it did not contain any practical measures towards the restoration of democracy in the kingdom. The political parties did not participate in the 1981 elections over the plea that the political system did not provide an appropriate atmosphere for their participation, that there was no political freedom and that ban on political parties had continued.

In the 1986 elections to the National Panchayat, the Nepali Congress, despite a strong resentment among its cadres, continued to follow policy of electoral boycott. On the other hand, many of the outlawed political parties participated in the elections and registered a satisfactory performance. For instance, the communists secured 16 seats. Actually the Nepali Congress leadership was strongly divided over the issue of contesting the 1986 elections. One group was in favour of reconciliation with the king and believed that certain reforms could be introduced before the elections were held. But the other group did not agree to it and wanted to boycott the election. As a result, the party could not take a concrete decision and a situation of indecisiveness and confusion prevailed for sometime. The Nepali Congress leaders were invited by the government to discuss the issue of freedom of speech, impartial atmosphere in elections, ban on political parties, etc., raised by it but talks were failed. The party's belated decision to keep itself away from the elections had resulted in a revolt among its cadres who were in favör of participating in the elections. A number of party members decided to contest the elections independently. The party cadres were more frustrated because initially they had been instructed to prepare themselves for the election. Lateron, the party could not launch a nationwide campaign to convince people about its stand.

The reforms in the panchayat system had proved to be inadequate from the point of view of the political parties as the partyless character of the system continued. After the 1980 panchayat elections the democratic leaders understood clearly that it was not possible to actualize the goals of democracy through reform measures. Hence, a strong movement was required to overthrow the panchayat system.

1990 Movement for Democracy

The 1990 movement for the restoration of democracy was a net outcome of the polarization of various parties and political groups in Nepal. There was a realization among the political parties that it was not possible to overthrow the panchayat system without a nation wide movement. It was also realized that it needed support of all the political forces. The need for a united struggle was felt by both the Nepali Congress and the United Left Front. The efforts of the Nepali democratic forces were highly encouraged by the world wide resurgence of democracy. The Indian political leaders also encouraged their Nepali counterparts in launching a united struggle for democracy.[17]

The main objective of the movement was to replace the panchayat system by a multi – party democracy. The Nepali Congress convention of January 1990 was the beginning of the movement. The most significant thing about the movement was that most of the political parties, professional organizations, associations and students joined it. And it was for this reason that despite atrocities of the panchayat government it took up a nationwide shape. The intensity of the movement was realized when even the government officials began to join the movement in a big way. King Birendra ultimately decided on 8th April 1990 to dissolve the panchayat government and withdraw ban from the political parties. On 16th April the king declared withdrawal of the panchayat system and declared to replace it by a multi – party democracy. The democratic forces accepted it and the movement ended.

Working of Democracy in the Post 1990 Period

After the abrogation of the Panchayat system an interim government was constituted under the leadership of K.P. Bhattarai of Nepali Congress in which other political parties were also given representation. The first general elections to the 205 – seated House of Representatives took place on 12 May 1991. The radical communist forces of the country decided to boycott the constitution under the banner of Nepal Communist Party (Unity Centre). They were demanding for the abolition of the constitutional monarchy and declaring Nepal a republic. 43 political parties participated in the general elections. The Nepali Congress and the United Marxist-Leninist Party (UML) were the largest among them. They also had the advantage of being at the forefront of the movement for the restoration of democracy in the country. The National Democratic Party (NDP) constituted by the earlier panchayat stalwarts had an image of being a traditionalist party, although it also advocated for multi party democracy in the changed situation. The various political parties focused on strengthening democracy, development and an independent foreign policy but they were not free from internal dissensions and leadership conflicts.

Only 7 political parties registered a victory in the elections. The Nepali Congress emerged as the largest party with 110 seats and the UML as the largest opposition party (69). The Nepali congress formed the first elected government under the Prime Ministership of G.P. Koirala. K.P. Bhattarai the Prime Minister of the interim government lost the election and as a result his claims as the leader of the elected government narrowed down severely.

Working of the NC Government

The new government was suppose to work for the realization of the aspirations of the people and also the objectives of the 1990 democratic movement. Not only that there was the task to lay down a strong foundation of democracy but it was also essential to activise the developmental process in the kingdom in order to realize popular needs and aspirations. The Koirala government did try to prepare a programme to meet basic requirements of the people such as :

Free education for all up to secondary levels,

Abolition of dual ownership of land,

Welfare of squatters and landless people,

Establishment of health centers in villages,

Linking each district headquarters by road transportation, and

Providing communication facilities in villages

Apart from its obligations to realize the goals of the 1990 democratic movement the Nepali Congress government also wanted to adopt popular measures in order to strengthen its base. However, it was not an easy task. There were serious problems within the party. The Bhattarai faction was not happy with the leadership of Koirala. The organizational and the governmental wings of the party were opposed to each other. Koirala government was accused of ignoring the party organization in taking important policy decisions. He was also criticized for being ineffective in the disposition of governmental functions. The internal party disputes greatly.

The oppositional political parties took advantage of the internal differences of the Nepali Congress. Both the UML and the Unity Centre opposed the government on the issues of civil servants strike, Tanakpur barrage agreement, price rise of essential commodities, etc. The interest of UML and the Bhattarai group within the Nepali Congress coincided and they began to pressurise the Koirala government. There were clear indications that the UML and the anti Koirala group within the Nepali Congress could unite together to pressurise the government. Towards the middle of 1994 there were also rumours regarding the non-confidence motion being tabled against the government. Taking these developments into consideration, Koirala resigned in August 1994 before the motion could have been actually registered. The parliament was dissolved on his recommendation and fresh elections were declared. Thus came an end to the first elected government. It was indeed not an encouraging development. The working of the first elected government was largely constrained due to leadership clashes, oppositional politics and it resulted in instability and non-performance. It is a fact that some sincere efforts should have been made by the government towards the strengthening of democracy but the functioning of the government resulted in political instability and disorder.

Mid – Term Elections

The second general elections took place in November 1994. The Nepali Congress party participated in the elections along with lot of intra-party rifts. There was not much change in the issues that the political parties had raised in the 1991 elections but in terms of party's performance there were decreasing trends. Actually, the political parties did not have much to offer to the people in the form of raising issues as a part of their election campaign. The Nepali Congress was particularly in a disadvantageous situation because the internal clashes within the party were largely responsible for premature elections. The UML was beneficiary in the sense that it had an issue to point out and it was the non-performance of the Nepali Congress party. The hardcore communists seemed disappointed with the democratic process. Hence, they decided not to participate in the elections. The United People's Front which had secured 9 seats in the 1991 elections remained out of electoral fray.

In the mid-term elections no political party could secure a majority. The UML emerged as the largest party with 88 seats and the Nepali Congress remained number two with 83 seats. The NDP secured 20 seats and the NSP 3. The UML formed a minority government under the leadership of Man Mohan Adhikari with the support of other smaller political parties from outside.

Working of the UML Government

It was for the first time in the history of Nepal that the communists got an opportunity to form a government. Although it was a minority government The UML government took certain populist measures such as "build our village ourselves" (BOVO) programme, allowance (Rs. 100) to old people, welfare programme for the landless and depressed communities, development of health facilities and irrigation facilities. The UML party tried to strengthen its position in the rural areas. It also wanted party's domination in various government bodies. Hence, a large number of appointments were made from among the party cadres in the government bodies, commissions, embassy's etc. Despite being a minority government it also took steps towards politicization of media, educational institutions and higher positions in the administration. As a result, the UML government invited opposition from the Nepali Congress, NDP and NSP.

Unstable Governments

In may 1995 the opposition political parties moved a non-confidence motion against the UML government. Prime Minister Man Mohan Adhikari resigned and recommended dissolution of the parliament. The parliament was dissolved and fresh elections were declared by the King. However, his decision was challenged in the Supreme Court and the court ordered reinstallation of the parliament. It was argued that before the Prime Minister had recommended dissolution of the parliament, the non-confidence motion had already been registered against the government. Hence, his request was not valid. The parliament was revived in September 1995. The Nepali Congress formed the government under the leadership of Sher Bahadur Deuba with the support of NDP and RPP. This time the Nepali Congress decided to handover Prime Ministership to second rank leadership, as there were strong differences among the top leadership of the party. However, Sher Bahadue Deuba faced strong opposition from his own party as well as the opposition political parties particularly UML. Though Deuba was a compromise candidate among the top leadership of the party, he was believed to be close to K.P. Bhattarai. Hence, Koirala group was not happy with the government. Deuba government was charged with corruption and inefficiency. The Maoist insurgency had begun by this time and his government was also criticized for being unconcerned to the Maoist problem. The Deuba government survived a non-confidence motion in March 1996. but had to step down in March 1997.

In March 1997, the UML-NDP and NSP formed another coalition government under the leadership of Lokendra Bahadur Chand of NDP. This coalition could not survive for more than six months. It was replaced by another coalition of UML-NDP-NSP under the leadership of Surya Bahadur Thapa of NDP. Interestingly both Lokendra Bahadur Chand and Surya Bahadur Thapa of NDP enjoyed Prime Ministership with only 19 seats of their party in the parliament. The Thapa government started facing strong opposition from the Nepali Congress and he had to quit in April 1998.

Nepali Congress once again began to search possibilities for the formation of a new coalition government. Incidentally towards the end of 1997 after the local bodies elections, the UML had splitted with 40 MPs under the leadership of Bam Deo Gautam and C.P. Mainali to form a new political party, called CPN-ML. The Nepali Congress and ML reached to an understanding to form a coalition government. While the Nepali Congress was in search of a new partner, the CPN-ML wanted to enhance its position against the CPN-UML. G.P. Koirala became the Prime Minister. The two coalition partners had reached to the understanding that the Prime Ministership will go to the other coalition partner after six months. However, in December 1998 Koirala refused to handover Prime Ministership to the CPN-ML. The two partners also developed differences over several other issues. The CPN-ML issued a 25 point programme which included increase in the members of his party in the cabinet, opening the Kalapani issue, etc. Prime Minister Koirala did not accept these demands. On 10 December 1998 13 CPN-ML members of the cabinet resigned. The ML decided to table a motion of non confidence against the Koirala government. The UML came to the rescue of the Nepali Congress not so much because it was willing to support the party, but mainly because it wanted to let down the CPN-ML. Koirala resigned, the parliament was dissolved and fresh elections were declared for May 1999. The NC-UML-NSP national government was formed till the elections were completed.

The coalition governments were the bitterest experience of the post-1990 Nepali politics. It not only resulted in political instability but also reduced the prospects of the strengthening of democracy in the country. There were a number of problems with the coalition government and their partners. It can be said that the political parties were largely responsible for the failure of the coalition experiment and political instability.[18] They were more concerned about wielding power. Nevertheless the existing socio-political conditions, the destabilizing role of the feudal – authoritarian forces, non-fulfillment of the basic needs of the people and deteriorating economic conditions were the equally responsible factors.

1999 General Elections

The third elections to the House of Representatives were held in two phases on 3rd and 17 May 1999. The Nepali Congress was the only party to nominate its candidates all the seats of the lower house. The UML nominated 194 candidates and CPN and ML for 197 seats. On the whole 41 political parties participated in the elections. Interestingly, 13 political parties placed only one candidate each in the elections.

In the 1999 elections the Nepali Congress projected K.P. Bhattarai as the candidate for Prime Ministership. Koirala group agreed that if the party would gain majority and Bhattarai would win the election he would be the Prime Minister of the country. Thus, the party tried to reach to a consensus and it appears that the party was of the conscious internal dissensions fluids it was faced with and wanted and tried to resolve them as much as possible.

The Nepali Congress emerged as the majority party in the elections with 110 seats. The CPN-UML had emerged as the main opposition party with 67 seats, NDP 11, NSP 5, Jana Morcha 5, United Jana Morcha 1 and NMKP 1. Interestingly, the CPN-ML could not register victory on a single seat. K.P. Bhattarai won the first election of his life and as per internal understanding of the party he became the leader of the parliamentary party.

Political Instability and Challenge to Democracy

It was not very late that the Bhattarai government began to face criticism from its own party cadres. The government was charged for ineffectiveness, and adopting an indifferent attitude towards the Maoist problem, etc. Since December 1999 Koirala group began to appose the Bhattarai government. They started to pressurize K.P. Bhattarai to resign from the government. Koirala group became so impatient that it ultimately threatened that if Bhattarai would not tender his resignation a non-confidence motion would be tabled in the parliament against the government. Bhattarai resigned in February 2000. Thus the pressure tactics of Koirala proved fruit bearing. But the things were not smooth for Koirala as well. In fact, Sher Bahadur Deuba had also claimed for the leadership of the parliamentary party. The tangle between Koirala and Deuba had to be resolved through voting in which Koirala won by 69 votes against 43 in favour of Deuba. G.P. Koirala became Prime Minster in March 2000. Koirala's second phase of Prime Ministership was marked by a number of developments. His government was charged for widespread corruption. The Maoist problem had aggravated by this time. Koirala government could not take any concrete steps towards the resolution of the problem. On June 1, 2000 King Birendra and his whole family was assassinated. The Koirala government was accused for being cool on this issue. He was also being targeted by the opposition political parties.

Koirala had to resign in July 2001 and Sher Bahadur Deuba took over as the Prime Minister of the Nepali Congress government. Deuba was serious about the resolution of the Maoist problem. Earlier also he had headed a committee constituted during the tenure of Prime Minister Bhattarai for the resolution of the Maoist problem. Prime Minister Deuba persuaded the Maoists for a ceasefire and peace talks with the government. Three rounds of talks were held between the government and the Maoist leaders between August-November 2001. However, the Maoists did not agree to anything less than the formation of a Constituent Assembly, a republican state and a new constitution for Nepal. The government was however, not prepared to accept any of these demands. The talks failed and the Maoists again resorted to violence.

On 26 November 2001, a state of emergency was declared in Nepal. The army was deployed in order to bring the Maoists under control. The emergency was extended in February and May 2002. Deuba had no doubt made sincere efforts towards the resolution of the Maoist problem, but there was no agreement on the basic issues. None of the parties were prepared to compromise. In May 2002 Deuba resigned and the parliament was dissolved. It was decided to hold fresh elections in November 2002 on a phased basis.

Assertion of Monarchy

Before the fresh elections could be held king Gyanendra dismissed the Deuba government in October 2002. Deuba had suggested that due to the Maoist insurgency it was not possible to hold general elections in time. But the king did not agree to his suggestion and dismissed his government. The king himself wanted to play an active role in politics.

After the dismissal of the elected government, king Gyanendra nominated Lokendra Bahadur Chand of NDP as Prime Minister with a small cabinet. The larger parties like Nepali Congress and CPN-UML did not join the government. In Mid 2003 Chand was replaced by Surya Bahadur Thapa. But Thapa also failed in resolving the problems posed due to the Maoist insurgency. The Pressure was mounting on king to return back to the democratic process. In mid 2004 he again appointed Sher Bahadur Deuba as the Prime Minister of Nepal. Deuba had been dismissed in 2002 and now by appointing him as Prime Minister King wanted to show that he was concerned towards the restoration of democracy. But actually king Gyanendra just wanted to pacify the international pressure. King Gyanendra took a drastic step in February 2005 by dismissing the Deuba government and himself assuming all political powers. Gyanendra's decision was a set back to democracy in Nepal.[19] Nevertheless, it opened doors for the polarizations of Maoists and the political parties. In fact the royal coup of 2005 led to three major political developments in Nepal : the Maoist ceasefire, alliance between major political parties and understanding between political parties and the Maoists. The April 2006 movement for the restoration of democracy was an outcome of these developments. The movement not only opened doors for the restoration of democracy but the Maoists also gave up insurgency and joined the mainstream politics to work for the establishment of a new democracy in the country.

CONSTITUTIONAL DEVELOPMENT IN NEPAL

The constitutional history of Nepal began towards the end of the decade of forties in a highly fragile way. Nepal's first attempt towards a short of a constitution was the government of Nepal Act 1948, which was drafted but could not be implemented. Since than Nepal owned 6 constitutions till 2008. A brief overview of these constitutions would give us an understanding of the nature and direction of constitutional development in Nepal.

The Government of Nepal Act 1948

It was the first attempt by any Nepalese rules towards providing a short of a constitution to the people of Nepal. It was not expected of the authoritarian Rana rulers to introduce any political reforms. However, in the context of the growing discontent against their rule, the British withdrawal from the sub continent on which the Ranas had relied much for support and the dawn of democracy in the South Asian region with the abandoning of the colonial rule, the Rana rulers considered it wise to take up a reformist approach.

The Rana Prime Minister Padma Shumsher JBR who framed the government of Nepal Act viewed it as a scheme of political reforms aimed at realizing his aspirations of reforms in the country.[20]

The act provided for fundamental rights such as freedom of person, speech, liberty, press, assembly, worship, equality. The executive powers were vested upon the Rana Prime Minister. There was a provision for a council of ministers to assist the Rana Prime Minister in administrative works and to be appointed by him. The act also provided for a legislature divided into two parts: the panchayats divided into gramin (village) and nagar (city) panchayats. Direct elections were to be held for gramin or nagar panchayats. Secondly, the central legislature consisting of two houses: Rashtra Sabha and Bhardar Sabha. Rastra Sabha consisted of 60-70 elected (by Panchayats) and nominated members in the ratio of 2:3. The Bahardar Sabha consisted of 20-30 members nominated by the Rana Prime minister.

The central legislature was a permanent body but it was provided in the constitution that one – fourth of the members would retire every year. The bills passed by the legislature were subject to their ratification by the Rana Prime Minister through his signatures.

The Act also provided for a judicial system. It was stated that the elementary civil and criminal justice shall be administered by the panchayats. It also provided for Courts and Courts of Appeal and a High Court. The Act also made provisions for the universal free and compulsory elementary education, with an objective to liquidate illiteracy. A provision was also made in the Act for the formation of a public Service Commission.

Rana Prime Minister Padma Shumsher abducted before the Act could be promulgated and his successor Mohan Shumsher refused to implement it. Thus the government of Nepal. Act 1948 could not be implemented. It may be pointed out here that the need for a constitution was felt by the Rana ruler taking into consideration his personal interest.

The Interim Government of Nepal Act 1951

The Interim Government of Nepal Act 1951 came into operation after the withdrawal of the Rana rule. The idea was that certain rules and regulations were required to streamline the politics and the administration till a constitution was framed and promulgated.

It was stated in the interim constitution that the government will work for the improvement of social conditions of its people, make effective provisions for securing right to work and education, to public assistance in cases of unemployment, old age, sickness and disablement and to improve living standard of the people in general and weaker sections of the society in particular. The constitution also provided for equal opportunity, rule of law, personal liberty and prohibition of trafficking in human beings, beggary and other forms of forced labour.

The executive powers were vested on the king. It provided for a council of ministers headed by a Prime Minister to assist the king in the execution of his powers and functions. The Prime Minister and members the cabinets were appointed by the king. King was also the supreme commander of the defence forces of Nepal. King had the sovereign power to make laws for the country. The cabinet could submit a bill for the consideration of the king, who could assent to the bill, hold it or return it. The constitution also provided for an Advisory Assembly consisting of the members nominated by the king.

The Act also made provision for the constitution of an Election Commission. The Election Commission was entrusted with the task to prepare electoral rolls.

Aim of the interim government was stated as to create conditions as early as possible to hold elections for the parliament.

1959 Constitution

This Constitution was framed by a commission constituted by the king on March 16 1958. The constitution was promulgated by king Mahendra on February 12, 1959. The 1959 constitution made provisions for a wide range of fundamental right to the people of Nepal in the sprit of a democratic constitution. These fundamental rights included personal liberty, equality, religion, and property, freedom of speech, assembly, association, residence and right to constitutional remedies.

The executive powers were vested on His Majesty who would exercise powers through a council of minister headed by the prime minister. It was maintained that His Majesty shall act on the recommendation of the cabinet. The prime minister was to be appointed by His Majesty and other ministers on the recommendation of the Prime Minister.

There was also – provision for a Council of State consisting of President and Deputy President of Senate, Speaker and Deputy Speaker of the House of Representatives, minister and such other persons appointed by His Majesty. The functions of the Council of State were: proclamation of the accession of His Majesty's successor in accordance with the law, custom usage in Nepal and arrangements for Regency if king was a minor or unable to perform his duties.

The 1959 constitution also provided for a Parliament consisting of two houses: Senate and the House of Representatives.

The Senate consisted of 36 members – 18 elected by the House of Representatives and 18 nominated by His Majesty. The term of Senate was six years.

The House of Representatives consisted of 109 members elected on the basis of universal adult suffrage. The House of Representatives did not have powers to discuss any issue relating to the conduct of His Majesty and also relating to the conduct of Chief Justice and other judges of the Supreme Court. The bills passed by the house could become law after receiving royal assent to it. His Majesty could withhold his assent to a bill; return it along with his observations.

His Majesty had the powers in the constitution to declare emergency in the country in case of threat of war, internal aggression or a grave economic crisis. His Majesty would assume all powers in such a situation. He could also assume emergency powers in case of failure of constitutional machinery and suspend any provision of the constitution pertaining to part III, IV & V. His Majesty could also suspend either or both houses of the parliament and him assume the law making power.

Part VI of the constitution made provision for a Supreme Court headed by a Chief Justice appointed by the king in consultation with the Prime Minister.

The constitution also vested upon His Majesty powers to enact, amend and repeal a law relating to the succession to the throne. He was also the Supreme Commander of the armed forces.

General elections were held in Nepal for the first time in February 1959 on the basis of this constitution. However, the newly installed parliamentary democracy was abrogated by king Mahendra in December 1960 and the constitution was also withdrawn.

1962 Constitution of Nepal

After the abrogation of the parliamentary democracy king Mahendra took over all powers in his hands and established his direct rule. He argued that the parliamentary democracy based on the western models of governance was not suitable to the Nepalese conditions and had proved to be a failure. He therefore began to search a 'third world model' of democracy suitable to Nepalese culture, history and traditions. He followed the footsteps of Gen Ayub Khan of Pakistan, Sukarno of Indonesia and Col. Naser of Egypt and envisaged a new system of governance for Nepal called panchayat system.

The 1962 Constitution maintained that the governance of the country in consonance with the popular will was only possible through a partyless democratic panchayat system, which was rooted in Nepalese traditions. Hence it was stated to be an indigenous system.[21]

The constitution defined Nepal as an independent, indivisible and monarchical Hindu kingdom.

The panchayat constitution made provisions regarding citizenship that every person who had his domicile in Nepal and:-

(1) Who was born in Nepal; or

(2) Either of whose parents was born in Nepal; or

(3) Who, as a women, had any kind of relation with a citizen of Nepal constituting matrimony in accordance with the laws and customs of Nepal; or

(4) Who had already obtained a certificate of citizenship in accordance with the laws of Nepal; shall be a citizen of Nepal.

Part 3 of the constitution was related to fundamental duties and rights. The fundamental duties of the citizen of Nepal were stated as devotion and loyalty towards the kingdom of Nepal; exercise one's rights with due regards to the law and without infringing upon the rights of others; to follow the system established under the constitution and to maintain social harmony. The fundamental rights prescribed in the constitution were: right to equality, right to freedom, right against exile, right against exploitation, right of religion, right of property and right to constitutional remedies.

The constitution also prescribed a number of restrictions on the exercise of fundamental rights relating to national security, law and order, peace and harmony and prevention of internal or external disturbances.

The constitution vested sovereignty of Nepal in His Majesty and provided that all powers – executive, legislative and judicial emanate from him. The constitution provided for a council of ministers appointed by the His Majesty to aid and advises him in the execution of executive powers.

A four tier panchayat system was established viz village or town assembly and village or town panchayats, district panchayats, zonal panchayats and National Panchayat. Direct elections were held only at the lowest web of the paqnchayat hierarchy. The constitution also provided for a Raj Sabha, Supreme Court and other courts.

The 1962 constitution was amended thrice in 1967, 1975 and 1980. In 1967 post of Prime Minister was created to head the council of ministers and the Back to the Village National Campaign was given a constitutional status. In 1975 amendment class organization system was introduced. Its objective was stated as to promote popular welfare, social harmony and people's participation. Six class organizations prescribed in the constitution were: Nepal Women's Organization, Nepal Peasants Organizations, Nepal Youth's Organization, Nepal Election Organizations and Nepal Ex–Servicemen's Organizations.[22] The 'Zone of Peace' Proposal was included in the constitution as one of the goals of foreign policy. The Prevention of Abuse of Authority Commission was also formed in this amendment. The 1980 amendment included appointment of the Prime Minister on the basis of the recommendation made by the National Panchayat, direct election to the National Panchayat on the basis of adult franchise and abolition of the Back to the Village National Campaign.[23]

The 1962 panchayat constitution remained effective till 1990 when the panchayat system was abrogated after a nation wide democratic movement. It was replaced by a multi party democratic system.

The 1990 Constitution

The 1990 constitution envisaged for a constitutional monarchy in Nepal. It declared Nepal as a multiethnic, multilingual, democratic, independent, indivisible, sovereign, Hindu and constitutional monarchical Kingdom. The sovereignty was vested in the Nepalese people and exercised in accordance with the provisions of the constitution.[24]

The constitution provided for wide ranging fundamental rights to the Nepalese citizens viz right to equality, right to freedom, right to press and publication, right regarding criminal justice, right against preventive detention, right to information, right to religion, right against exploitation, right against exile, right to privacy and right to constitutional remedy. The constitutional also narrated directive principles and policies of the state.

His Majesty the king of Nepal was regarded as the symbol of Nepalese nationality and the unity of the Nepalese people. He had exclusive powers to enact, amend or repeal the law relating to the order of succession to the throne by the descendents of His Majesty. The constitution also made provision for a Raj Parishad.

The executive powers were vested in His Majesty and the council of Minister headed by a Prime Minister. The leader of the majority party in the House of Representatives was appointed as Prime Minister by His Majesty.

The legislature consisted of to two houses: House of Representatives and National Assembly. The National Assembly or upper house consisted of 60 members : 10 members nominated by His Majesty, 35 members (including at least three women) elected by the House of Representatives on the basis of proportional representation by means of single transferable vote, 15 members – 3 each from five development regions elected by single transferable vote by an electoral collage consisting of the Chief and the Deputy Chief of the village and town level local authorities and the Chief and the Deputy Chief and the members of the district level local authorities.

The House of Representatives consisted of 205 members elected on the basis of adult franchise.

The constitution vested powers relating to justice in an independent judiciary consisting of Supreme Court, Appellate Court and District Courts. The constitution made provisions for a number of commissions such as Commission for the Investigation of Abuse of Authority, Public Service Commission, Election Commission, etc. All the political parties / organizations were required to register with the Election Commission. Any party based on religion, community, caste, tribe or region was not recognized by the Election Commission. Any political party contesting election to the House of Representatives was required to have at least five percent women candidates out of its total candidates contesting the election.

The emergency powers vested on His Majesty. He was also the Supreme Commander of the royal Nepal Army.

The 1990 constitution was replaced by the Interim constitution promulgated in January 2007.

The Interim Constitution 2007

The basic objective of the interim constitution has been to provide a set of rules and regulations for the governance of the country till it is replaced by a permanent constitution.[25]

The preamble of the interim constitution for the first time used the words "we the people of Nepal, in exercise the sovereign powers and state authority inheritent in us"........

The sovereign authority is vested in the Nepalese people. The constitution has declared Nepal as an independent, indivisible, sovereign, secular, and inclusive and a fully democratic state. While Nepali is the official language all the languages spoken as the mother tongue in Nepal are the national languages of Nepal.

Regarding citizenship the interim constitution states that the following persons who have their domicile in Nepal shall be deemed to be citizens of Nepal by decent:

(a) A, person who has acquired citizenship by decent before the commencement of this constitution.

(b) Any person whose father or mother is a citizen of Nepal at the birth of such person.

(c) Any person born till the end of mid April 1990 and has been permanently residing in Nepal shall acquire the citizenship of Nepal by birth as per the laws in force.

The interim constitution also provides for fundamental rights to Nepalese citizens such as right to freedom, equality, right against untouchability and social discrimination, right regarding publication, broadcasting and press, right regarding environment and health, education and cultural right, right regarding employment and social security, right to property, right of women, right to social justice, right of child, right to religion, right to justice, right against preventive detention, right against torture, right to information, right to privacy, right against exploitation, right regarding labour, right against exile and right to constitutional remedy.

Responsibility of the state is stated to be to conduct free and impartial election for the members of the Constituent Assembly, to ensure progressive socio – economic and political change in the country, etc.

The executive powers are vested in the council of Ministers and executive functions of Nepal will be carried in the name of the government of Nepal. The Prime Minister and the council of ministers shall be constituted on the basis of political consensus reached between Seven Party Alliance and NCP (Maoist) on November 8, 2006. The Prime Minister and the Council of ministers are responsible to the Legislature – Parliament.

The Interim Constitution had also provided for a 330 member Legislature – Parliament consisting of 209 members of SPA and other parties who had elected members in the 1999 parliament: 73 members of NCP (Maoist) and 48 members from Sam Yukta Bam Morcha, intellectuals, professionals, etc.

The membership of the Constituent Assembly was raised to 601 through an amendment with 240 members elected through First Past the Post System, 335 to elect on the basis of proportional representation and 26 nominated from the civil society.

The Judiciary Consists of Supreme Court, District Courts and Appeliate courts.

The constitution also provides for Commission for Investigation of Abuse of Authority, Public Service Commission, Election Commission and National Human Rights Commission. The constitution provides that the Supreme Commander of the armed forces will be appointed by the council of minister and the armed forces will be responsible to the council of ministers. It also makes provisions for a National Defense Council.

The emergency powers are also vested in the council of ministers and in case emergency is declared due to external or internal reasons it shall have to be placed before the Legislature – Parliament within one month.

It is essential for all the political parties to register themselves with the Election Commission. Any party, acting against the sprit of the preamble of the constitution will not be registered with the Election Commission.

The Constituent Assembly has to frame the new constitution in two years time.

Constitutional Development in Nepal: An Assessment

Nepal has a constitutional history of more than half a century. But its experience with constitutionalism has been highly fragmented and disappointing. Nepal has so far 6 constitutions. But the constitutional development has not been unilenear. Every time with the change of the political system a new constitution came into operation. The 1948 Act was not implemented. 1951 was an interim constitution but remained effective for 8 years. The 1959 constitution was based on the model of constitutional monarchy, but the parliamentary system established on its basis could not been sustained and was abrogated within a short period of time.

The Panchayat constitution of 1962 in a way uprooted the process of democratization initiated since 1950. Nepal returned back to the authoritarian rule of monarchy under the cover of democracy. The panchayat system although claimed to be an indigenous model of democracy, with its partyless character and absolute concentration of powers in the hands of the king, it proved to be a façade of democracy.

The 1990 constitution reinstalled constitutional monarchy in the country. The 1990 constitution no doubt brought parliamentary democracy to the country but monarchy remained at the centre of politics. Hence it was semi - constitutional monarchy.

What is most important in the context of constitutional development of Nepal is that the Rana Prime Minister in the case of 1948 Act and monarchy in case of other constitutions had been the source of constitutions. Constitutions have been framed by the Constitution Making Committees appointed by the king. It was never framed by a Constituent Assembly. The sovereign power had vested with His Majesty. The only exception to these practices has been the interim constitution of 2007, which states that the sovereign power rests with the people of Nepal.

In all the past constitutions emergency powers rested with the monarchy and the monarchy misused it to himself take over the power on one pretext or the other.

The democratic forces had very little role to play in the framing of the constitutions. Even in 1990 the Constitution Making Committee was reframed after a strong resistance by the political parties. None of these constitutions offered scope for an inclusive democracy.

On the whole it can be said that although Nepal had several constitutions in the past, they were neither based on popular sovereignty and popular will nor they strengthened democratic process in the country. The panchayat constitution which remained effective for 28 years promoted royal political supremacy and authoritarianism. One may say that despite constitutions a strong foundation of constitutionalism could not be laid down in Nepal. It is for this reason that after a more than half of a century's journey of constitution Nepal is once again heading for a new constitution. But one may add here that after a long struggle the political circumstances are changed in Nepal to begin the process of framing a new constitution.

Summing Up

The Nepalese people have witnessed several ups and down in their journey to democracy and constitutionalism. There have been several changes during the last half a century. In one way the process of democracy may be characterized as one step forward and two steps backward. Actually, ever since the 1950 revolution, the traditional political elite represented by the monarchy had always occupied the centre stage of politics. As a result of this the democratic elite never got an independent hand in framing a constitution and building democracy in the country.

After the 1950 revolution the political parties had to share power with the monarchy and the Ranas in the name of a middle way approach to democracy. The political parties which had a narrow social base got fragmented and it paved a way for the assertion of the traditional political elite. The feudal order of the society and backward economic conditions favoured authoritarianism more and the democratic process lesser.

The democratic process failed in Nepal due to the political assertion by the king and the strong bases of authoritarianism in the country. The panchayat system also uphold the political supremacy of the monarchy. It tried to create a confusing situation by disallowing the political parties in the political process and propagating the panchayat system as the indigenous model of democracy. But the panchayat rulers failed in understanding the democratic impulses of the Nepalese people. Hence the panchayat system scumbed to the 1990 democratic movement.

The reinstallation of democracy was a highly significant development but the political process in the post 1990 period failed in stabilizing democracy in the country. It became clear that it was not sufficient to create constitutional and political superstructures.

The reassertion of political power by monarchy after 2001 in a gradual but determined manner and the royal coup of early 2005 lead Nepal to a yet another democratic movement in 2006. The Nepalese people have perhaps now learned that a sound basis for the stabilization of democracy and constitutionalism can not be crated unless the objectives conditions in which democratic government has been working are not substantially changed. Therefore, in the post 2006 phase the main issues of the Nepali politics became restructuring of state, inclusive democracy and socio – economic reform agenda.

References

1. For details in this regard refer to Bhuwan Lal Joshi and Leo E. Rose, *Democratic Innovations in Nepal, A Case of Political Acculturation,* California University Press Berkeley, 1966; Anirudha Gupta, *Politics in Nepal* 1950-60, Kalinga Publications, Delhi, 1993; Bhola Chatterji, *A Study of Recent Nepalese Politics,* The World Press, Calcutta, 1967.

2. M.S. Jain, *The Emergence of a New Aristocracy in Nepal,* Sri Ram Mehra & Co., Agra, 1972; Adrian Server, *Nepal Under the Ranas,* Oxford & IBH, New Delhi, 1993.

3. Kanchanmoy Majumdar, *Political Relations Between India and Nepal* 1877-1923, New Delhi, 1973.

4. Kanchanmoy Majumdar, *Nepal and the Indian Nationalist Movement,* Firma K.L. Mukhopadhyay, Calcutta, 1975.

5. See, K.P. Karunakaran, *India in World Affairs* 1950-53, Oxford University Press, Delhi, 1958; Bhola Chatterji, *n.1.*

6. Anirudha Gupta *n.1*:155.

7. H.M. King Mahendra, *Proclamations, Speeches and Messages,* HMG, Kathmandu, 1967; p. 2.

8. Bhola Chatterji, *Nepal's Experiment with Democracy,* New Delhi, 1977: 99-100.

9. HM. King Mahendra, *n. 7.*
10. See for these explanations, Margret W. Fisher and Leo E. Rose, *The Politics of Nepal: Persistence and Change in An Asian Monarchy* Cornell University Press, Ithaca, 1971: 51-52.
11. Joshi and Rose, *n.1.*
12. See, Rishikesh Shah, *Nepal Politics, Retrospect and Prospect,* Oxford University Press, New Delhi, 1978; Sangeeta Mathur, *'Panchayat System in Nepal,* Unpublished Ph.D. Thesis, University of Rajasthan, Jaipur, 1995.
13. See for Details, Borgh Erik Borgstrom, *The Patron and the Panca,* Vikas Publishing House, New Delhi, 1980; B.C. Upreti, "Back to the Village National Campaign in Nepal", paper presented at a seminar in Centre for the Studies of Nepal, BHU, Varanasi, March, 1979.
14. See for the constitutional measures taken in this direction, L.S. Baral, "Changing Constitutional and Political System of Nepal", *Foreign Affairs Report* (New Delhi), January, 1977.
15. B.C. Upreti, "Nepal's Panchayat Democracy in Crisis", *Eastern Economist,* January 25, 1980: 187.
16. See, D.P. Kumar, *Nepal : A Year of Decision,* Vikas Publishing House, Delhi, 1980; Rishikesh Shah, *Politics in Nepal 1980-90,* Manohar, Delhi, 1990.
17. B.C. Upreti, *The Nepali Congress, A Study of Party's Performance in 1991 General Elections and Its Aftermeath,* Nirala, New Delhi, 1993:
18. See for a Study of party politics during the Nineties, Lok Raj Baral (ed.), *Nepal, Political Parties and Parliament,* Adroit Publishers, Delhi, 2004.
19. B.C. Upreti, *Nepal Democracy At Cross Roads,* Kanishka Publishers Distributors, Delhi, 2007.
20. See Bhuwan Lal Joshi and Leo & Rose, *no. 1*
21. Rishikesh Shaha *no. 12.*
22. *The Rising Nepal,* December 13, 1975.
23. *The Rising Nepal,* December 16, 1980.
24. See, 'Preamble', *text of the Constitution of the kingdom of Nepal* 2047, HMG, Kathmandu, 1990.
25. *Interim constitution of Nepal* 2063 (2007) Kathmandu, 2007.

2

Prelude To Constituent Assembly Elections

In the recent political history of Nepal the formation of constitution recommendation committee and the promulgation of the constitution has been a privilege of the monarchy. The need for a Constituent Assembly was never realized though the demand for a Constituent Assembly was raised by the Communist Party of Nepal as early as 1950. There was an understanding in 1950 that a permanent constitution will be framed by a Constituent Assembly. But none of the political groups and actors raised this issue. Than what lead to the holding of elections of the Constituent Assembly in 2008 is a significant issue. The formation of the Constituent Assembly is not related to the framing of a constitution alone. It has already set a direction to the emerging state and political order in Nepal. As such the question of Constituent Assembly is closely associated with the recent political transformations in Nepal.

This chapter intends to discuss the political developments leading to the election of the Constituent Assembly.

During the panchayat era the main agenda before the democratic forces was restoration of the democratic order in the country. The political parties and the organized political activities were banned under the panchayat system. Therefore, the survival of the political parties rested on the establishment of a democratic system. As a result the struggle of the political parties was confined to the restoration of democracy in the country. The demand for the restructuring of the state and formation of the Constituent Assembly elections were essentially the post 1990 developments emanating in the context of the Maoist movement.

The 1990 democratic movement was an outcome of the joint struggle of different sets of political parties and groups in Nepal. However, the constitution making process after the abrogation of the panchayat system repeated the history. There was some resistence regarding the formation of the constitution making committee and it was reconstituted on that basis, but the need for a Constituent Assembly was not accepted and the constitution was framed by the Committee itself.

Maoist Movement and the Demand for CA

The radical communist groups of Nepal had participated in the 1990 democratic movement with an objective to abrogate the panchayat system and open doors for the establishment of a broad based democratic system. The hardcore communist participated in the 1991 general elections under the banner of the Unity Centre and emerged as the third largest party in the Parliament.[1] But they were frustrated with the working of the parliamentary democracy in the subsequent years for three reasons : failure on the part of the political parties in attaining governmental stability and good governance, continuation of the political influence of the traditional elite particularly the political assertion by the monarchy and the governments apathy towards addressing itself to the issues of socio – economic reforms. The hardcore communists took up a confrontationist approach towards the government. They decided not to participate in the 1994 mid term elections and started preparing for a nationwide violent movement.

The Maoist movement began in February 1996. In its 40 point demand charter the Communist Party of Nepal (Maoist) included demand for a new constitution to be drafted by the people's representatives, declaring Nepal a republican state and a new democracy in the country. The Maoists had a firm opinion that an inclusive democracy was not possible in Nepal unless a new constitution was promulgated by the people themselves through their representatives. Hence, the Constituent Assembly formed the core of the Maoist demands.[2]

The Maoists intensified their protracted war after 1996 in a gradual but steady manner. They not only consolidated their organizational strength but also expanded their area of influence particularly in the countryside. Apart from their protracted Guerrilla war against the state the Maoists also used the instrument of peace negotiations in order to realize their political goals. They declared a ceasefire on 23

July 2001, two days after Shere Bahadur Deuba had been appointed new Prime Minister of Nepal. It may be pointed out here that Deuba had been earlier involved in negotiations with the Maoists. Prime Minister K.P. Bhattarai had constituted a committee under the chairmanship of Sher Bahadur Deuba to suggest ways and means for the resolution of the Maoist problem. The Deuba Committee submitted its report on 7 November 2000. It agreed that there were problems with the structure of the Nepali state and the system of governance in the country. It suggested looking into the root causes of the Maoist insurgency. But the committee did not state any thing regarding the Maoist demand for the restructuring of state and the framing of a new constitution. Earlier Prime Minister Lokendra Bahadur Chand had constituted a committee under the chairmanship of communist leader Prem Singh Dhami in April 1997, to suggest for the resolution of the Maoist problem. Dhami Commission though talked of the need to bring the Maoists in the political mainstream and introduce socio – economic reform it also did not refer to the Maoist political agenda. So none of the political parties were willing to open its mind regarding the Maoist demands for the republican state and the Constituent Assembly. It is true that the question of republican state was complex and none wanted to take a risk in the context of the prevailing political scenario in the country. But they also did not talk of the Constituent Assembly as well.

Sher Bahadur Deuba was much enthusiastic about finding a solution to the Maoist problem. It is true that earlier he had been involved in the peace making efforts but the fact was that he had been selected leader of the parliamentary party by the Nepali Congress due to a conflict among its top ranking leadership. So he wanted to establish that he was capable to find out a solution of the Maoist problem. Another important point is that after the June 2001 royal massacre Gyanendra had assumed the throne and he was in search of a political legitimacy. The Maoists had taken an aggressive posture after the sad demise of King Birendra. They had expressed the view that after king Birendra's brutal murder monarchy had come to an end in Nepal. Therefore king Gyanendra was looking for support from various quarters. He also wanted to show that he was concerned to peace and stability in Nepal.

Three round of peace talks were held between the government and the Maoists between August – November 2001. These peace talks, however, failed as the government was not prepared to accept the Maoist demands of republican state, Constituent Assembly and new democracy. The Maoists were on the other hand not prepared to accept any thing less than restructuring of state and a new constitution framed by the Constituent Assembly. The 2003 talks between the Maoists and the government also failed as the government had no mood to concede the Maoist demands.

These peace initiatives failed in finding any solution of the Maoist insurgency. However, the Maoists succeeded in strengthening their political position. They could also take a firm position on the issues that they had been taking about viz. republication state and a new constitution for Nepal framed by the Constituent Assembly. It also helped them to make the people of Nepal aware of these issues.

The political situation in Nepal began to take a sharp turn with the royal coup of February 1, 2005. It gave an opportunity to the Maoists to change their political strategy. At the same time the political parties also began to realize that the monarchy was the main obstacle to the stabilization of democracy in the country.[3] This realization brought the political parties and the Maoists on a common platform. The Maoists demands for the restructuring of state and society began to receive a broader space with the growing Maoist understanding with the political parties. In fact, the post February 2005 political developments were highly significant in building an atmosphere for a political change in Nepal and developing a broader acceptance to the demand for elections to the Constituent Assembly. In fact, the Maoists had realized that it was not possible to attain their political objectives merely through an insurgency. In the changed context a democratic approach appeared more feasable.

Post Royal Coup Political Developments

King Gyanendra's royal coup of February 2005 was aimed at consolidating political powers in his hands and at the same time to put the political parties and the Maoists under pressure. But Gyanendra's calculations did not favour him and it went the other way round. The king lost domestic and international sympathy and support and on the other hand it brought the political parties and the Maoists on one platform. It opened doors for the subsequent polarization of democratic forces and Nepal's transition to democracy and the restructuring of the state. An overview of these developments here would be helpful in understanding the context of the Constituent Assembly elections in Nepal.

Gyanendra's Assumption of Powers

King Gyanendra dismissed the Sher Bahadur Deuba government on 1 February 2005 and declared a state of emergency in the country. In his announcement the king said that he himself would assume all powers and rule the country directly as Chairman of the council of ministers for a period of three years.[4] He took advantage of the constitutional provisions under article 19 of the 1980 constitution, which provided for emergency powers to the king. However, Gyanendra's action was uncalled for as there was no such urgency for declaring emergency in the country. The kind of situation prevailed in the country had continued for last many years and there was nothing extra ordinary. Secondly, many scholars believed that the king's action was not in accordance with the spirit of the 1990 constitution.[5] It was not clear as what was the justification behind announcing his direct rule for three years? It was clear that the king was highly ambitious. He wanted to become a real power holder. But no one would have thought of such a drastic and early action by king Gyanendra. The Royal Nepali Army assisted the king in the implementation of his political motives. The civil rights provided in the 1990 constitution were suspended.[6]

King Gyanendra's assumption of powers followed a series of actions against his political adversaries. The main political leaders were house arrested or detained or placed in jails. All kinds of communications, media, and radio and television services were brought under control. The media persons, intellectuals and other persons of the civil society who had been supporting the cause of democracy were also arrested or they were compelled to not to move outside their city or district. Gyanendra alleged that the political parties had failed in containing violence, controlling corruption in the country and improving economic situation. He also blamed that the political parties did not take any serious step towards controlling the Maoist problem. He was not happy with the working of the political parties. Gyanendra also alleged that the government had failed in holding the general elections. King was perhaps trying to held political parties responsible for all kind of violence and disorder in the country and at the same time he was trying to justify his own action.

King Gyanendra tried to create a support base for himself. The Royal Army was already supporting him. He decided to seek assistance from the old guards of the panchayat era. On 2 February king announced a 10 member council of ministers. On 14 February he appointed Tulsi Giri and Kirti Nidhi Bisht as Vice Chairman of the council of ministers. He brought back those leaders of the panchayat era who had been out of active politics since long but who had been strong supporters of the monarchy. Thus the king tried to return to the panchayat era.[7] He also took a number of administrative measures with an objective to consolidate his powers.

Towards the middle of the year he announced withdrawal of the emergency. But control over media, communication, etc. continued. Actually, it was done just to satisfy the international community, which was pressurizing the king to return to multi-party democracy. The king continued with its absolute control over the state power. He also tried to seek support from the international community in the name of controlling the Maoist insurgency. India, USA, UK and the other donor countries to Nepal though not happy with the action of king Gyanendra, continued to support him so as to bring the Maoist insurgency under control. Nepal also sought support from China, Pakistan, Russia, etc.

The government had begun to consolidate RNA attacks on Maoists after the royal takeover. The Maoists also retaliated in a big way and attacked the government establishments at several places.[8]

King Gyanendra announced that the Maoists should surrender their arms and return to the mainstream politics. It was made clear that those who would follow this direction would be rewarded and those who do not agree to it would face military action. He was, however, not prepared for any negotiations with the Maoists. The Maoists called for a 3 days strike in February 2005 and than 11 days long strike in April 2005. The Maoists and the king were aware of each other's intensions and goals and hence, there was no possibility of any understanding between the two.

Seven Party Alliance

King Gyenendra adopted a confrontationist attitude towards the political parties and was not willing to negotiate with them. He blamed them, as pointed out earlier, for mis-governance, corruption and weakening of the process of national integration. King's actions against the leaders of various political parties further pulled them apart. The royal coup had already created a hiatus between the monarchy and the political parties. The disgusted political parties began to search possibilities for launching a united struggle against the king's takeover. In May 2005 seven political parties including NC, UML, NC (D), Janmorcha Nepal, NWPP, ULF, NSP (Anandi Devi) and NSP (AD) agreed to form an alliance to fight against the despotic rule of the king. The Seven Party Alliance (SPA) agreed on a 6 point programme that included restoration of the House of Representatives and the 1990 constitution, management of conflict, progressive movement for the restoration of democracy on the basis of 1990 constitution, adhearance to multi-party democracy and elections for a Constituent Assembly.[9] The SPA gave a call to do away with the autocratic rule of the monarchy. It accorded top priority to the restoration of the House of Representatives.

The Seven Party Alliance was the first major attempt of the political parties against the royal take over. It also paved a way for the polarization of democratic forces. It also gave a positive message to the civil society. On the whole it was a significant development and generated new hopes among the democratic forces, despite the criticism that it had chalked out a weak agenda.[10]

The Maoist Ceasefire

There was a positive change in the attitude of the Maoists. They began to realize that the political dynamics of the country was quite complex and the methodologies that they were applying were becoming doubtful in terms of realization of their political objectives. Despite a strong protracted war against the state the monarchy had brought itself to the centre stage of politics. The Maoists began to conceive that it was an opportune time to wage a gap between the king and the political parties who too were opposed to the king's action. King Gyanendra had viewed both the political parties and the Maoists as major obstacles to his direct rule. Thus in king's perception both were his political enemies. The political parties realized that the return to the multi party democracy was not possible without a struggle against the monarchy. This prompted the political parties to come closer to each other and also to look into the possibilities of joining hands with the Maoists.

The Maoists wanted to provide a larger space to SPA for the consolidation of its struggle against the king. So they declared a three months unilateral ceasefire, affected from September 2005. It was an important strategic move on the part of the Maoists because it created a difficult position for the king. It had build pressure on the government to respond to the Maoist ceasefire in a positive way. The government did not agree to do that. It argued that the

Maoists were not serious about peace and that the declaration of the ceasefire was only a strategy to strengthen their activities and programmes and streamline their organizational base. The Maoists succeeded in gaining the mass sympathy and confidence by declaring unilateral ceasefire.

It may also be noted here that the Maoist ceasefire also gave a positive message to the international community because king Gyanendra was trying to play the terrorist card in order to seek international support against the Maoists. The Maoists gave the message that they were interested in peace and conflict resolution and were not a supporter of terrorism and violence. The Maoist ceasefire helped in building confidence among the political parties and the civil society.

Need For a Joint Action

The Maoists and the political parties both were realizing the need to fight jointly against the royal takeover. King Gyanendra had though lifted emergency and there was some moderation in his attitude, it was clear that he was neither prepared to accommodate the democratic forces not there was any change in his attitude towards the Maoists or SPA. The Maoists had already shown their changing attitude by declaring a unilateral ceasefire. The Maoists and SPA were serious about reaching an understanding regarding the movement to be launched for the restoration of democracy. After a series of consultations among the leaders of the two groups and with the Indian leaders, it was agreed to work jointly for the restoration of democracy.

Maoist – SPA Understanding

On 17 November 2005 the Maoists and SPA agreed on a 12 point programme.[11] It emphasized re-structuring of the state for the establishment of absolute democracy in the country. There was an understanding to do away with the constitutional monarchy. The 12 points agreed upon were as following:

1. To establish absolute democracy by abandoning autocratic monarchic rule, thereby creating an appropriate atmosphere for a long term peace and stability.
2. Restoration of the House of Representatives, form an all party government and work towards holding elections for Constituent Assembly.

3. Bringing an end to armed conflict through a dialogue and seek international mediation for this purpose.
4. Expressing commitment to democratic norms, and values and complete faith on multi party democracy, civil liberties, human rights, rule of law and the fundamental rights.
5. The CPN (Maoist) expressed its commitment to create a congenial environment for the installation of democracy by allowing political activists of various political parties to return to their earlier positions, who had been displaced during insurgency.
6. The CPN (Maoist) expressed its commitment not to repeat past mistakes.
7. The Seven Party Alliance expressed its commitment to not to repeat past mistakes, while in the government.
8. Respect to the norms and the values of human rights and press, freedom of press and move ahead accordingly.
9. Boycott of the forthcoming municipal elections as the king announced them with selffish motives.
10. Commitment to protect the independence, sovereignty, geographical integrity of the country and national unity. Maintenance of peaceful relations with all countries based on the principle of peaceful, co-existence and good neighbourly relations with the neighbouring countries.
11. Call to civil society, professional organizations, diverse communities and regions, intellectuals and the media to participate in the peaceful movement to be launched on the basis of understanding between the political parties and the Maoists.
12. To settle any problem emerging between the two through peaceful dialogue at the concerned level or at the leadership level.

Restoration of Democracy

In March 2006 it was decided to launch a movement for the restoration of democracy. The Maoists withdrew a 20 days economic and transport blockade scheduled from March 14, 2006 at the request of SPA. The movement that was finally initiated in April against the direct rule of the king received widespread support from all walks of the civil society. It was clear that the monarchy had lost popular faith. It was for the first time that the monarchy was denounced by the political parties and the people. The movement launched by the Seven Party Alliance had full backing of the Maoists. King tried his best to curb the movement. Curfew was imposed in Kathmandu. But it could not prevent the people from organizing widespread demonstrations against the king. The crackdown on the masses by the government further agitated the people. King was abused and denounced like a common man.[12] He was infact, badly exposed and there was a strong internal pressure on him. King's policy of suppression was not fruit bearing. He also came under strong external pressure and ultimately had to concede to step down.

India played a significant role in persuading different political groups in Nepal to work in favour of democracy.[13]

Reinstallation of the Parliament

King Gyanendra could not resist the pressure of democratic forces and after 18 days agitation he declared to restore the 1999 House of Representatives and hand over power to the leader of the Seven Party Alliance.

What compelled the king to withdraw? Actually, king Gyanendra had tried to defuse the democratic forces and also to keep the political parties and the Maoists apart. But the two forces had come together. It was not possible to withstand their pressure for long. The king was also under pressure of the international community. India had already suggested the king to restore the parliament. There were clear indications that the monarchy was loosing its respect and importance and that the people were becoming highly critical of king Gyanendra's role. It is also said that the dissatisfaction was gradually brewing up among the armed forces, while the king was dependent on the support of the armed forces.

The Seven Party Alliance favoured restoration of the 1999 parliament but the Maoists did not appreciate it as they believed that it would delay Nepal's heading towards the goal of elections for the Constituent Assembly. They alleged that the Seven Party Alliance was betraying the people's movement.[14] The Maoists were in favour of an all party conference in place of the restoration of the parliament. They believed that they were being sidelined by SPA in this regard and that their support for the April movement was not fruit bearing to them.[15] Later on they agreed to it. SPA elected G.P. Koirala of the Nepali Congress Party as its leader. Madhav Nepal leader of UML declared that "the announcement of Constituent Assembly elections will be the main agenda of the reinstated parliament.[16]

SPA – Maoist Agreement

The negotiations of the Seven Party Alliance with the Maoists finally reached to an eight point agreement along with a code of conduct. The agreement included framing of an interim constitution, establishment of an interim government, which would take up the task to conduct elections for the Constituent Assembly, issues relating to disarming the Maoist forces, future of the Maoist army and peace building. The code of conduct included the cessation of armed Maoist forces in rural areas, release of the Maoist prisoners by the government, disbandment of parallel government of the Maoists and return of the underground Maoists to overground.[17] This agreement was important as it formed a basis for the subsequent negotiations between the Maoists and SPA.

SPA formed a new government under the Prime Ministership of G.P. Koirala. The positions distributed to the constituents of SPA in the council of ministers were : CPN – UML-6, NC-7, NC(D) – 4 and one each to ULF, NSP and Jana Morcha.

An important issue that comes here is that what lead to the change in the approach of the Maoists? It appears that the Maoists had realized that in the upcoming political changes in Nepal it was possible to join hands with the democratic forces. It was not possible to continue with the arms struggle and than the outcome was not certain. The political parties were willing to join hands with the Maoists as the king had now become a common enemy of the two. The Maoists thought that it was an appropriate time and an opportunity to advance their political agenda through democratic means.

Issue of Arms Management

The question of the Maoist arms management was important in taking the peace process further due to many reasons. There was an impression in Nepal that the peace process would not proceed further unless the issue of arms possessed by the Maoists and their armed forces was settled properly. It is true that the Maoists and SPA had undergone an understanding to work together for the restoration of peace and democracy in the country But both the groups were of the opinion that the settlement of the question of arms management was vital.

In the summit talks held between Prachanda and G.P. Koirala on 8 October 2006 it was agreed that CA elections would be held in June 2007. The issues relating to arms management, etc were also discussed. It was also said that if the CPN-4M2 did not cooperate they would move ahead on their own. SPA constituents later unanimously agreed to the six point agreement signed with the Maoists.

Six Point Agreement

The six point agreement concluded between SPA and the Maoists on 7 November, 2006 reaffirmed their commitment to work together for peace, stability and democracy in Nepal. It was also agreed that all the agreements concluded earlier would be implemented. The charges leveled against the Maoist leaders were withdrawn and it was agreed to release all the political prisoners. The Maoists and SPA also agreed for the management of army and arms, finalization of the interim constitution, interim legislature, interim government, the future of monarchy and other issues. It was a comprehensive agreement and the understanding relating to the Maoist army, interim constitution and elections for CA were important as they had been the cause of concern for both since June 2006. The CPN-UML though one of the signatories to the agreement added its note of dissent stating that the fate of monarchy should be decided by a referendum along with the elections of the CA and that proportional system should be adopted for the elections of the CA.

The management of the arms occupied by the Maoists and their combatants was an important issue as the peace process and further political steps towards the CA elections would rest on it. The government and the Maoists succeeded in resolving this issue despite initial confusion. The process of arms verification and registration of the Maoist combatants began in February 2007 under the supervision of a UN team and continued in different phases till the end of 2007.

Comprehensive Peace Accord

The comprehensive peace accord of 21 November 2006 conveyed full commitment of the Maoists and the government of Nepal to build peace, democracy and stability in the country. It stated that no authority relating to governance will rest with the king. All property possessed by late king Birendra and his family was to be nationalized and be placed under a trust. It stated that all property of king Gyanendra received by him in the capacity of the king of Nepal will be nationalized.

Both the parties agreed to strengthen multi-party competitive democracy and resolve the issues relating to gender, ethnic, dalit and regional identities. It also mentioned about management of the Maoist arms and the armed forces as per earlier agreement concluded. Both sides agreed to abandon all kind of activities that would create a war like situation and expressed their determination to realize peace in the country. The agreement declared an end to the armed conflict. Adhearence to human rights, fundamental rights of the people of Nepal and humanitarian laws was also expressed. It also added to economic and social rights along with political rights of the people.

One significant aspect of the accord was that: "Both sides agree to become responsible and accountable in a personal and collective way and not to repeat further mistakes committed in the past and also to correct these mistakes on a gradual basis"

The agreement appealed to the civil society, the professional groups, the class organizations, the media, the intellectual community and all the Nepali people to actively participate in building a new Nepal and establishing lasting peace through the elections to the Constituent Assembly by ending the armed conflict.

The peace accord was significant as it paved a way for the settlement of the pending political issues. It also gave a message to the Nepali masses that serious efforts were being made towards peace and stability in the country. It was a confirmation on the part of the Maoists that they were prepared to end armed conflict and join the multi party democracy along with the other political parties.

Actions Against the King

One important dimension of the post April 2006 politics of Nepal was to withdraw powers of the king and make the monarchy ineffective in the politics of the country. There has been a strong opinion that king Gyanendra and his associates had done lot of atrocities on the people during his direct rule. The interim government took a number of decisions to besieze the king. It was declared that the king would no more be the head of the state and the chief of the army. The Raj Parishad was abolished. The reinstated parliament curtailed the king's privileges. It ended the concept of king in parliament. The requirement of royal assent to the bills was withdrawn. King's assets were brought under the review of taxation. The Nepali Congress was though still toeing with the idea of a ceremonial monarchy[18], the Maoists were not prepared to make any compromise with regard to the institution of monarchy.

The Government constituted a commission under the Chairmanship of justice Krishna Jung Raimajhi to recommend action against 202 people including king Gyanendra. Justice Krishna Jung Raimajhi submitted its report to the government on 20 November 2006. The commission held king Gyanendra responsible for the atrocities on the people at the time of April 2006 pro-democracy movement. It was also recommended that action be taken against king Gyanendra not in his capacity as the king but as the then head of the state. The chairman of the committee said, "We have decided to recommend the parliament to take necessary steps against the king as we found him guilty."[19] It was also clarified that though king Gyanendra did not respond to the questions send by the commission it does not mean that he did no do any wrong. It is for the first time that a commission was constituted. against the king of Nepal.

A five-member committee was constituted to recommend action against the king. The monarchy lost all its credibility. It can be said that the role played by king Gyanendra had proved to be detrimental to the status, prestige and powers of the institution of monarchy in Nepal. It seems that king Gyanendra in his capacity as the head of the state had to pay for all that happened during his direct rule. Not only that his powers were withdrawn but the facilities provided to him were also curtailed. His personal property was under scrutiny, the monarchy lost powers and popularity. It was also decided that the monarchy would be abolished if the king was found conspiring against elections to the CA.[20] The king and members of the royal family were also asked to declare their property and provide details about their personal accounts in banks in Nepal and abroad.[21] In the budget for the year 2007-2008 it was decided not to provide any allowance to the king and the members of the royal family[22] Earlier there was a provision of an allowance of Rs. 18.7 million for the king and the royal family.

The Interim Constitution

We have already pointed out various significant features of the interim constitution of 2007 in the previous chapter. Here only some references have been made to the provisions of the constitution relating to the structure of the Constituent Assembly.

The interim constitution initially provided for the constitution of a 425 member Constituent Assembly as following (before amendment):

1. 202 members of the Constituent Assembly to be elected directly from the existing parliamentary constituencies on the basis of First – Past the Post System.
2. The political parties were to nominate 204 members in proportion to the votes they would score in the election to the Constituent Assembly.
3. 16 members were to be nominated by the council of ministers.

Every Nepali who has attended 18 years age was given right to vote in the election to the CA. The time accorded to the CA for the framing of the constitution was 2 years from the time of its constitution. However, the election date scheduled for June 2007 was postponed to 22 November 2007 and again to April 10 2008.[23] The Constituent Assembly has to perform dual functions: as a constitution making body and as a legislature for the interim period.

The interim constitution was amended for the first time on March 9, 2007 to accommodate the demands of the people of Tarai. It was decided to grant proportional representation in all state organs to Madheshis, Dalits, ethnic groups and backward castes.[24] A Constituency Delimitation Commission was also constituted lateron. The second amendment to the interim constitution was introduced in April 2007. It was concerning the abolition of the monarchy by two third majority of the interim parliament if he would be found indulging in sabotaging the elections to the CA.[25] In another amendment the membership of the Constituent Assembly was raised to 601: 240 on the basis of FPTPS 335 on the basis of Proportional Representation and 26 members were to be nominated from civil society.

Maoists in the Interim Government

The peace process in Nepal covered one major landmark with CPN (Maoists) joining the interim government on April 1, 2007.

Actually the Maoists were expected to join the government earlier but due to the unsettled political issues there was an over all delay in all aspects of political life in Kathmandu. It was, however, a positive development that despite delay the Maoists were persuaded to join the interim government.

G.P. Koirala resigned as Prime Minster and the interim parliament again appointed him as Prime Minister of the interim government. The speaker of the house, Subhash Kumar Newang read the proposal on behalf of the eight parties (SPA and CPN (Maoist) to reappoint Koirala as Prime Minister.[26] Koirala became Prime Minister of Nepal for the 6th time. Two significant aspects of the cabinet formation were that for the first time the king did not administer the oath of office to the members of the cabinet. Similarly, for the first time oath was taken in the parliament in stead of the Narainhity Royal Palace as earlier.

The interim government consisted of 21 members including 16 cabinet ministers and 5 ministers of state. The Nepali Congress received 4 cabinet positions namely, defense, home, finance and peace and reconstruction; the CPN (Maoist) got 5 including information and communication, local development, physical planning and works, forest and women the UML got 5 cabinet ranks and our minister of state and Nepali Congress (D) three cabinet ranks and one minister of state.[27] The Maoists joining the interim government included Hisila Yami (Comrade Parvati) wife of Maoist leader Babu Ram Bhattarai and President of all Nepal Women's Association (Revolutionary). Hisila Yami had been closely associated with the Maoist protracted war.

The newly formed interim cabinet outlined its main objectives as holding elections to the Constituent Assembly, establishing law and order in the country and promoting economic development. The formation of the interim government was highly praised by the political leaders. Prakash Man Singh, Vice President of the NC (D) said "The Constituent Assembly would now draft the political future of the country". The Maoist supremo Prachanda also said: "Once we entered mainstream politics following the cease-fire, we were prepared to form a new Nepal. So we have come prepared to shoulder responsibilities for the sake of the nation".[28]

The violent movement erupted in the Tarai in the beginning of 2007 delayed the peace process. The Tarai groups were not happy with the meagre representation of the region. They were also not happy with the Maoists as they thought that they were not pleading the cause of inclusive democracy and federalism.[29]

Political Uncertainty and Suspicious

The Maoists wanted to resolve the questions relating to the republican state, CA and monarchy as early as possible. They thought that delay would generate more complexities. The Maoists had problems for a number of reasons. They alleged that the government did not consult them while making various appointments. They were not happy with king Gyanendra's defending his earlier actions on the democracy day of Nepal and the king's birthday bash.[30] The Maoists were also suspicious about Koirala's stand on the future of monarchy. He had in fact, created confusion by taking different stands at different points of time. The Maoists also had the fear that the royalist forces could play a disruptive role and create problems in smooth conduct of the CA elections.

In June when elections to CA were postponed for November 2007, the Maoists began to demand for declaring Nepal a republican state before the elections. The Nepali Congress stand was that it could be done by CA only. The Maoists threatened to start yet another movement. The Maoists were also worried about the non-response to their demand of adjustment of the Maoist combatants in security forces. They also threatened that if this issue along with the problem of adequate facilities in the Maoists army camps were not resolved they would not cooperate with the second round of arms verification.

The Maoists submitted a 22 point demand charter to the government, which included abolition of monarchy, declaring Nepal a republican state before holding elections to CA and proportional representation election method for all the seats of CA. It may be recalled here that it had already been decided in the interim constitution that half of the seats of CA would be elected on the basis of proportional representation. Why Maoists wanted a change in the electoral system is an important issue. It is a fact that the Maoists, both as a revolutionary group engaged in protracted guerrilla war and as a partner with SPA involved in peace process, had established the fact that they were a political force to be reckoned with. Now they were worried about their political future within the democratic political set up of the country. The delay in the elections to the CA was a serious issue for the Maoists as the political future of the country would rest upon it. The Tarai agitation had weakened the base of Maoists in that region.

The Maoists declared on 18 September 2007 to leave the interim government as the government did not agree to their demands. A Maoists leader said, "We have pulled out from the government on September 18 as the talks failed to reach an understanding on the immediate abolition of monarchy and a proportional electoral system"[31] It was serious blow to the peace process in Nepal. However, the Maoist leader Mahara made it clear in a statement that "Now we will focus on peaceful protests to meet our demands".[32]

The decision taken by the Maoists added to the political uncertainties in the country. They clearly said that they would not join the government again unless their demands were met with. The Maoists had also talked of waging a nationwide movement in order to create a momentum for federal democratic republic. 87 member of the parliament led by the Maoists registered an application at the PM office to call a special session of the parliament to amend the constitution to change the election system of the CA.[33]

Yet another set back to the peace process was the decision of the government on October 5 to postpone the elections of CA indefinitely.[34] This decision of the government was not unexpected in the context of their differences with the Maoists. It was feared that Maoists could boycott the elections if they were to be held on the scheduled date. But what is unfortunate is that it could not been possible to hold elections to the CA for a year.

The CPN (UML) and two other left parties registered their note of dissent over the issue of postponing the CA elections. The civil society and the international community also expressed its displeasure over the decision of the Nepali government. The Indian view point was that it affected the credibility of the government and also disturbed the process of democratic transformation and legitimization in the country.[35] The United Sates of America and Britain also expressed their displeasure over the dicision of the Nepali government.[36] Similarly China also expressed its concern over the postponement of the CA elections. The chief of UNMIN, Ian Martin called upon the Maoist leaders and urged them to be soft on their demands. It shows that the international community was also concerned over the postponement of the elections. The general impression was that the postponement of the CA elections for a longer time period could be counter productive.[37] Hence efforts were immediately made to reach to some understanding with the Maoists. The demands raised by them were discussed in the parliament in November 2007. There was, by and large, a consensus on the issue of the republican state. But the government made it clear that it would only be done by the Constituent Assembly. The peace process was derailed between October – December 2007. But both the Maoists and the government had shown enough resilience. They were engaged in negotiations all the time. It appears that the political groups in Nepal learned from the circumstances. The civil society had become much more active to resolve the tangle.

December 2007 Agreement

The Maoists and the government finally reached to an agreement on 23 December 2007, which brought the peace process back on the track once again. It can be said here that both the groups had exhibited political maturity and determination. In fact, despite several ups and downs, at no stage efforts were left aside to come to the negotiation tables. It was decided to hold the CA elections on 10 April 2008.[38] Taking all issues to consideration it was agreed to keep the strength of the CA to 601 seats : 240 to be elected on the basis FPTP system on the basis of proportional representation and to be nominated by the council of ministers. It was also agreed to declare Nepal a republican state but the formal declaration was to be made in the first meeting of the Constituent Assembly. The Maoist joined the government again in early 2008 and the process of elections to the Constituent Assembly began subsequently.

Summing Up

It is clear from this brief discussion that the realization of the demand for the elections to the Constituent Assembly was closely associated with the Maoist insurgency in Nepal. During the initial years of the insurgency there were doubts regarding the realization of the Maoists demands. The peace talks had failed and the government was not prepared to concede any of the demands of the Maoists including elections for the Constituent Assembly. But the internal political dynamics of Nepal brought a drastic change. The royal coup of February 2005, the Maoist ceasefire; the polarization of democratic forces; the Maoist – SPA understanding and the decision of the Maoists to join the mainstream politics proved to be the major landmarks in the realization of the objective of the formation of the Constituent Assembly.

References

1. See, B.C. Upreti, *The Nepali Congress*, Nirala Delhi 1993; Laxman K.C., *Recent Nepal*, Nirala, Dehi,: Michael Hutt (ed.), *Nepal in Nineties*, Oxford University Press, Delhi, 1993; Martin Hoften et.al. *People, Politics and Ideology, Democracy and Social Change in Nepal*, Mandala Book Point, Kathmandu, 1999.

2. For a detailed discussion and references see, Arjun Karki and David Seddon (eds.), *The People's War in Nepal, The Left Perspective*, Adroit Publishers, New Delhi, 2003; Deepak Thapa (ed.), *Understanding the Maoist Movement in Nepal*, Kathmandu, 2003; International Crisis Group, *Nepal's Maoists: Their Aims , Structure and Strategy*, Asia Report No.104, 27 October, 2005; Bishnu Raj Upreti, *Armed Conflict and Peace Process in Nepal*, Adroit Publishers, Delhi, 2006; Sambhu Ram Simkhada and Fabio Oliva, *The Maoist Insurgency in Nepal, A Monograph*, Geneva, March, 2006. Lok Raj Baral (ed.) *Nepal, Facts on Maoist Insurgency*, Adroit Publishers, Delhi, 2006, B.C.Upreti, *Maoists in Neal, From Insurgency to Political Mainstream*, Kalpaz, New Delhi, 2008.

3. B.C.Upreti, "Will Monarchy Survive" *SEMINAR*, 546, April, 2005.

4. For text of the speech delivered by king Gyanendra see, *The Kathmandu Post*, February 2, 2005.

5. Manjushree Thapa, "Nepal's Troubled Kingdom", *The Hindu*, April 23, 2006.

6. See, Michael Hutt, "Nepal and Bhutan in 2005, Monarchy and Democracy Can they Coexist?" *Asian Survey*, Vol. XLVI, No.1, January-February 2006:120.

7. Hutt, *n.6*: 121.

8. Uddhav P.Pyakurel, *Maoist Movement in Nepal: A Sociological Perspective*, Adroit Publishers, Delhi, 2007:118.

9. The Kathmandu Post, May 9, 2005.

10. B.C. Upreti, **n.1**:348.

11. *Nepal Weekly* (Kathmandu), Vol.6, No.15, November 20, 2005.

12. *The Hindustan Times*, April 24, 2006.

13. See, *The Hindustan Times*, April 20, 2006; Nilobia Roy Choudhary, "The Great Indian Balancing Act," *The Hindustan Times*, April 23, 2006.

14. *The Hindu*, April 26, 2006.

15. International Crisis Group, *Nepal's Peace Agreement: Making it Work*, Asia Report No. 126. December 15, 2006:3.

16. *The Hindustan Times,* April 26, 2006.
17. Sita Ram Yechuri, "Learning From Experience, An Analysis of Approaches of Maoists in Nepal and India", *Economic and Political Weekly,* April 9, 2005.
18. Amit Dhakal, "Koirala Advocates Ceremonial Monarchy", *The Hindu,* June 15, 2006.
19. *The Hindu,* June 15, 2005.
20. *The Hindustan Times,* April 3, 2007.
21. *The Statesman,* March, 13, 2007.
22. *The Hindustan Times,* July 12, 2007.
23. *The Hindustan Times,* October 3, 2007.
24. *The Hindu,* March, 10, 2007.
25. *The Hindu,* April 11, 2007.
26. *The Hindustan Times,* April 2, 2007.
27. *The Hindu,* April 2, 2007.
28. *The Hindustan Times,* April 2, 2007.
29. See, International Crisis Groups, *Nepal's Troubled Tarai Region,* Asia Report No. 136, July, 9, 2007.
30. *The Hindustan Times,* July, 13, 2007.
31. *Asian News Digest,* October 20-26, 2007:6412.
32. *n.31*:6492.
33. *The Kathmandu Post,* September 29, 2007.
34. *Asian News Digest,* n.31: 6554.
35. http//*www.nepalnews.com.np*
36. *The Himalayan Times* (Kathmandu) October 6, 2007.
37. *The Himalayan Times* (Kathmandu) October 7, 2007.
38. *The Times of India,* December 25, 2007.

3

Electoral System And Election Management

In democratic political order a well defined system and the mechanism for holding elections is a must. In fact, the freedom and fairness of elections rests much on the electoral system. The efficient management of elections rests to a large extent, upon the electoral rules and regulations framed for conducting the elections. In this chapter we have planned to discuss some of the procedural issues and the mechanism designed for conducting elections to the Constituent Assembly.

The Election Commission

Let us first make out a brief overview of the Election Commission of Nepal. It may be pointed out here that in a democratic system Election Commission is the primary institution not only to conduct elections to the various representative bodies but also to ensure free and fair elections. It is the Election Commission which lays foundation for a broader popular participation and free and fair elections. It depends much on the autonomy and independence of the Election Commission. In democratic system the Election Commission enjoys autonomy with regards to the electoral mechanism and the election management. But the question of the dependence of the Election Commission on the executive for administrative reasons and the activities of the Election Commission being subject to judicial review pose limitations to its working. The question of autonomy of the Election Commission has been a crucial issue in a number of democratic systems.[1] The decisions of the judiciary the legislature, etc put limitations on the autonomy of the Election Commission.

The Election Commission generally depends on the executive for administrative assistance, security aspects, etc. The Election Commission is expected to act as a path provider to the entire electoral process in a country. Therefore, it is necessary that it is fully equipped to conduct its role. In all the democratic systems the Election Commission is entrusted with this task. Hence, the issues relating to its autonomy and independence remain significant.

The role of general elections in the evolution and development of the political system is a recent phenomenon in the context of Nepal.[2] For a considerably long time period Nepal was ruled by an authoritarian, absolutist and highly personalized rule.[3] Such a politico – administrative dynamics could have hardly opened any scope for the evolution of an electoral system of any form. It was after the abrogation of the Rana rule in 1951 that Nepal stepped on the path of democracy and adopted the modern electoral mechanism.

The interim government of Nepal Act 1951 for the first time provided for an Election Commission. It was stated that the King would appoint the Chief Election Commissioner with the advice of the cabinet. The Election Commission remained dysfunctional as Elections could not be held. The 1959 constitution did not make any separate clause for an Election Commission but there was a provision for the formation of an Election Commission. It was entrusted with the task to conduct the 1959 general elections. The Panchayat Constitution of 1962 did not make any provision for an Election Commission. However, in the first amendment to the constitution in 1967 part 13 (A) was inserted to make provision for an Election Commission.

The 1900 parliamentary constitution made provision for the formation of the Election Commission. The country had hold three general elections in 1991, 1994 & 1999.

The interim constitution in its part 14 provides for the Electicn Commission of Nepal.[4] The article 128 states that there shall be an Election Commission in Nepal consisting of a Chief Election Commissioner and up to four other commissioners. The Chief Election Commissioner and the other commissioners would be appointed by the Prime Minister on the recommendation of the constitutional council for a period of 6 years or up to the age of sixty five years. The interim constitution has laid down eligibility conditions for a person to be appointed as CEC or commissioners, as following:

(a) holds a Bachelor's degree from a University recognized by the government of Nepal.
(b) is not a member of any political party immediately before the appointment,
(c) has attained the age of 45 years, and
(d) has possessed high moral character.

The Chief Election Commissioner or and the election commissioners may be removed from the office on the same grounds and the same manner as the Chief Justice and judges of the Supreme Court. The interim constitution states that the government of Nepal shall provide all necessary administrative machinery and assistance to the election commission required for conducting the elections.

The immediate task of the Election Commission was to conduct elections of the Constitutent Assembly.

Provisions Relating to Elections

Voters

The act relating to electoral rolls states that a person with following qualifications would be eligible to vote in the elections to the Constituent Assembly:[5]

I. He is a citizen of Nepal.
II. Who has completed the age of 18 years on or before the last date of the "month of chaitra, i.e. 13 April of the year immediately preceding the year in which the electoral rolls are collected. The act further stated in the case of the election to the members of the Constituent Assembly, one who has completed 18 years of age on or before the last day of Mangsir of the year 2063 (December 15, 2006)" was eligible to vote in the CA elections.
III. Who has a permanent residence in the concerned ward of any village development committee or municipality in any election constituency?

The act provided that the name of a 'voter' shall be included in the electoral rolls of the election constituency where he is permanently residing and than registered in the electoral rolls.

A person of unsound mind or a person sentenced to imprisonment in pursuant to the laws in force relating to election offences or a person who is under imprisonment was not allowed to vote.

Preparation of Electoral Rolls

The act stated that the Election Commission was responsible for completing the task of preparing electoral rolls of the voters in the wards of the VDCs and municipalities of every election constituency. The Election Commission had to prepare these electoral rolls under its direct inspection, control, supervision and direction. The following provisions were made in the act regarding the preparation of electoral rolls:

I. Collection of information and inclusion / exclusion of voters in each ward of the VDC or the municipality.
II. Preparation of roll lists.
III. Publication of electoral rolls in the concerned wards of the VDC or municipality.
IV. Updating of electoral rolls, inclusion and omission of names. Removal of repeated names in the electoral rolls.
V. Final publication of electoral roll lists after completing the process of making claim, objection, holding enquires and making necessary amendments.

The act also provided that a separate temporary electoral roll may be prepared by the Election Commission to include the following:

(a) Employees serving in government offices, local bodies or organizations owned or controlled by the government of Nepal,
(b) Persons staying in army or police barracks or combatants of the Maoist army staying in cantonments,
(c) Prisoners and detainees in prisions,
(d) Employees and security personnel deputed in election works at polling centres.

The Act specified that the electoral rolls and temporary electoral rolls prepared shall not be admissible as evidence for other purposes except for the purpose of polling.

Election Constituencies for CA

Article 63 of the interim constitution provided for the following categories of members of the Constituent Assembly:

1. Two hundred forty members elected from two hundred forty election constituencies on the basis of the First Past The Post (FPTP) electoral system.

2. Two hundred forty members elected from the election constituencies set upon considering the entire country as a single election constituency for the election to be held under the Proportional representation System (PRS) where the votes will be allotted to the political parties on the basis of the votes secured by them under the first category.
3. Seventeen members to be nominated by the council of ministers on the basis of understanding from amongst the persons of high reputation who have rendered significant contribution in national life.

In the third amendment to the interim constitution in December 2007 the number of seats of the Constituent Assembly was raised 601, out of which the distribution of seats in the above mentioned categories was 240, 335 and 26 respectively.

Election System

The election system is the mechanism through which people exercise their right to vote. It is the method on the basis of which people exercise their right of political participation.

There was some initial confusion regarding the electoral system to be adopted for election to the Constituent Assembly. But finally a two fold system was adopted.[6]

First Past the Post System (FPTP): The phrase First Past The Post has been drawn from horse race. Actually in the horse race one who would cross the wooden post first is declared as winner. The same formula has been adopted in general elections. In this system in an electoral constituency a contestant seeking the highest number of votes is declared winner. It is also known as the plurality system. It means that there has to be a plural number of candidates and one candidate is declared winner among them. This system of election has been quite popular in India, USA, U.K., Canada, New Zealand, etc. In Nepal also 1959 and 1990 onward elections were held on the basis of this system. It is popularly known as the majority system. It provides mandate to one among the many aspirants to represent his voters, take part in legislative procedures and the government bodies.

The interim constitution states that; "the candidate securing the highest number of votes shall be elected as the member of the Constituent Assembly on the basis of one member in one election constituency from the election constituencies determined in pursuant to clause (a) of Section 3 under the First Past The Post Electoral System."[7]

The constitution also states that in this system one person may file nomination for maximum two constituencies. If such a person wons election from both the constituencies he will have to denounce membership of any one constituency in written to the chairperson of the Constituent Assembly within 30 days from the date of declaration of the election result. The seat thus fallen vacant shall be filled through by-election.

The constitution also states that while nominating candidates for this system the political parties should take into consideration the notion of inclusive democracy.

This election system has been quite popular and easy in operational terms. However, it is criticized on many counts. It is said that the representation of a party in the legislative body through this system does not always accurately reflect the popular support that the party may enjoy. For example a party may seek majority of seats in the parliament but the total votes it secured may be lesser. In 1991 general elections the Nepali Congress won in 110 seats in the 205 seated Parliament. But it secured only 33.4 per cent popular votes. It suggests that there was a gap between the percentage of seats secured by parties and the percentage of popular votes secured by it. It may also be noted here that in the 1999 general elections in Nepal the national political parties like Rashtriya Prajatantra Party (Chand) and Communist Party of Nepal (ML) could not secure a single seat. This system of election does not secure the interest of the minority political parties. Some times the political parties have higher percentage of popular votes secured but less number of the total seats secured by it. Therefore, it protects the interest of the dominant political parties only.

It has also been argued that the majority system works well where there exits the two party system. There is also problem of proper representation of women and various social groups in the plurality system.

Proportional Representation System

In the proportional representation a political party is given seats in the legislature in proportion to the votes secured by it in the elections. The parties put their candidates in the election and than seats are allocated to them in proportion to the votes it gained.

The interim constitution states that the persons representing under the Proportional Electoral System on behalf of a political party shall be elected to the Constituent Assembly in proportion to the number of total votes secured by such a political party. The votes will go to the political parties and the whole country shall be treated as a single election constituency.

It was also made clear that each of the contesting political parties will prepare a closed list of candidates. But those candidates who are contesting under the FPTP system can not be included in this list. It was also made clear that the political parties while preparing the closed list of candidates must keep in view the principle of inclusiveness and give proper representation to various groups such as women, dalits, tribals, Madheshis, etc.

Candidates and Nominations

The Act (2007) relating to the election of the members of the Constituent Assembly laid down the following qualifications for a candidate contesting election of the Constituent Assembly:[8]

1. He / She must be a Nepali Citizen.
2. He / She must have completed, 25 years of age.
3. The candidate must not have convicted of a criminal offence involving moral turpitude.
4. Must have not hold an office of profit. The office of profit means any position other than a political position for which remuneration is being paid out of a government fund.

It further stated that a person shall be disqualified to become a candidate in the election if:

(a) A person whose name is not inlisted in the electoral rolls.
(b) An incumbent office bearer of the government of Nepal of any organization that has been owned, controlled or receiving grant from the government of Nepal.
(c) A person who has not completed two years after released from jail.
(d) A person who has been prosecuted in the cause of corruption charges.
(e) A person who has been blacklisted by a bank or financial institution for being a defaulter.
(f) Mentally retarded person.

(g) A person who has been charged by the Probe Commission for abuse of authority, damaging public life, resources, human rights violation and misuse of treasury during 2006 democratic movement.

Electoral Offences

The Constituent Assembly Election Act 2007 also made provisions relating to electoral offences and violence.[9]

Adequate security of the polling stations, polling parties and other office bearers relating to elections and voters has to be ensured. Since the Election Commission does not have its won security personal it is the responsibility of the government. The returning officers were given powers to postpone polling of a polling station under special circumstances. In case of unauthorized seizure of polling stations, ballot boxes, damage to ballot papers or other voting devices, the Election Commission had power to cancel election in that polling both after proper scrutiny.

Electoral Expenses

The elections have become a costly affair to day due to the excessive use of money by the candidates and parties. It has in-fact become a common practice in many countries that the elections are won on the basis of money. So the money power has become a major factor in elections. How to control the use of money in elections has been a serious matter of concern for the Election Commission. The 2007 Act framed some rules relating to electoral expenses.

It was stated that the total expenditure by any political party or candidate shall not exceed the ceiling of expenses laid down by the Election Commission. The Election Commission fixed election expenses for each candidate. It was maintained that each candidate and party shall have to maintain a record of the electoral expenses and submit it to the Election Commission within thirty five days from the declaration of election results.

Registration of Political Parties

Political parties are the main vehicle of a democratic system. They are the main actors in the elections. It is the political parties which make democratic system operative. The working and stability of the democratic system depends much on the nature and dynamics of the political parties.

The interim constitution of Nepal states that persons who are committed to a common political ideology, programme and common philosophy are entitled to form and operate a political party of their choice. It states that the political parties with the objectives contrary to the spirit and norms of the preamble of this constitution shall not be considered qualified for the registration with the Election Commission.

Any political party willing to secure recognition of the Election Commission for the purpose of contesting elections is required to register its name with the Election Commission. The political parties seeking registration required to furnish the following details:

(a) Name of the political party and address of its head quarters or central office.

(b) Name of the leader and names and addresses of the members of its executive committee or any such other similar committee.

(c) The income sources of the political party along with its details.

The interim constitution states that the political parties shall have to meet the following conditions:

I. The constitution of the political party must be democratic.

II. It should make provisions for elections of the party office bears at least once in five years.

III. The party shall follow policy of inclusiveness in its membership. It means that there should be provisions for membership to tribals, backwards, dalits, women, etc.

IV. Party should ensure discipline among its members.

It has also been mentioned that a political party shall not be registered with the Election Commission if it does any discrimination in the distribution of its membership on the basis of religion, caste, tribe, language or sex. Similarly, the symbols of a political party should not be such which disturbs religious sentiments or communal harmony or integrity of the nation.

Each political party shall have to submit an application for registration along with a list of signatures of at least 10 thousand voters, who are the supporters of the party.

In the case of parties representing in the interim legislature this provision shall not be applicable.

The trends in the registration of political parties with the Election Commission in different election years shows that Nepal has followed a multi party system. It is also clear that the number of political parties gradually increased between 1991 to 1999. However, there is a decrease in 2007. It may be due to polarization of political groups both among the leftists, the rightists and the ethnic groups.

Table No – 1

Registered Political Parties

Year	*Parties Registered*	*Parties Contested*	*Candidates*
1991	44	20	1345
1994	65	24	1442
1999	100	41	2224
2007	74	55	FPTP = 3930 PR = 5891

Summing Up

No election can be conducted in a free and fair way without a proper structural arrangement for the management of the elections. The Election Commission is the primary instrument for holding the elections. In fact, it is the first requirement for holding elections in a free and fair atmosphere in a democratic set up. The question of autonomy of the Election Commission is also significant. There is also need for well defined rules and regulations regarding electoral rolls, voters, candidates, voting management, etc. The interim constitution and the various Acts relating to the Constituent Assembly elections made provisions relating to Election Commission and various laws and provisions required for the management of the elections.

One very significant feature of the Constituent Assembly elections was that for the first time Nepal adopted a dual procedure of elections: First Past The Post system and the Proportional Representation. This was done with a view to ensure representation of diverse groups communities and regions in the Constituent Assembly. So long Nepal had been holding elections on the basis of plurality or majority system. But it was realized that it had deprived many smaller parties and communities in seeking entry to the representative bodies. The Maoists had first raised the issue of broadening the procedure for representation in the Constituent Assembly.

Table No – 2

Polling Centres and Election Personnel

S.No.	*Year*	*Polling Centres*	*Polling Sub Centres*	*Election Personnel*
1	1991	8225	6504	62881
2	1994	7412	8191	74473
3	1999	6821	---	59490

Table No – 3

Registered Voters and Voting Percentage

S.No.	***Year***	***Registered Voters***	***Voting Percentage***
1	1991	1,11,91,777	65.15
2	1994	1,21,32,571	61.86
3	1999	1,35,18,839	67.00

Table No – 4

Percentage of Candidates for Cloud List

S.No.	*Groups to be Represented*		*Percentage of Candidates*
1	**Women**		50%
	Madheshis -----------------------	Women	15.6%
		Men	15.6%
2	Dalit -----------------------------	Women	6.5%
		Men	6.5%
3	Oppressed	Women	18.9%
	Tribes / Indigenous Tribes	Men	18.9%
4	Backward Region* -------------	Women	2%
		Men	2%
5	Others** ------------------------	Women	15.1%
		Men	15.1%

* Backward Region Means: - Achham, Kalikot, Jajarkot, Jumla, Dolpa, Bajhang, Mugu and Humla districts.

** Other means the group not clearly mentioned in this schedule.

The percentage is above 100 for the reason that a number of candidates representd more than one group.

Source: **Election Act** 2007

Table No – 5

S.No	Candidates Name	Madheshi		Oppressed-Tribes / Indigenous Tribes		Dalit		Backward Region		Others	
		M	F	M	F	M	F	M	F	M	F
1											
2											
3											
4											
5											
6											
7											
8											
9											
10											
11											
12											
13											
	Total Percentage										

Seal of the Person's Political Party

Authorized Signature

Source: **Election Act** 2007

Votes Cast for Each Political Party Assembly to Result Divisor Method

According to this method votes obtained by each contesting political party are divided by many dividers such as 1, 2, 3, 4, 5, 6, 7, 8, 9...... The result of such division is called quotient. After deriving quotient, the number of seats shall be allocated by dividing smaller ones from greater quotient until the seats are finalized. In making such allocation, even though a political party receives any votes whatsoever, the seats secured by such political party shall be allocated by being limited to the number of candidates enlisted by such party in the list.

For instance if there are 13 seats and five political parties the allocation of seats in accordance to the votes secured will be as following:

Table 6

Quotient	*Party A No. Votes 400000*	*Party B 100000*	*Party C 200000*	*Party D 50000*	*Party E 550000*
1.4	285714/2	71429/9	142857/4	35714/	392857/1
3					
5.					
7					
9					
11					
13					
Result	4	1	2	0	6

Source: **Election Act** 2007.

References

1. For an overview of the Indian experiences in this regard see, Anand Ballabh Kafaltya, *Democracy and Election Laws*, Deep and Deep Publishers, Delhi, 2003; Subhash C. Kashyap, **Blueprint of Political Reforms**, Shipra Publications, New Delhi, 2003.
2. See, Norman D. Palmer, *Election and Political Development, The South Asian Experiences*, Vikas, New Delhi, 1987.
3. See, Leo E. Rose and Margaret W. Fisher, *The Politics of Nepal, Persistence and Change in an Asian Monarchy*, Cornell University Press, Ithaca, 1970; Anirudha Gupta, *Politics in Nepal*, Kalinga Publications, New Delhi, 1990 (reprint), Rishikesh Shaha, *Nepali Politics, Retrospect and Prospect*, Oxford University Press, New Delhi, 1978.
4. *Interim Constitution of Nepal*, 2007: 64-66.
5. *Act Relating to Electoral Rolls* 2006, Act No 32, 29 December, 2006: 4-5.
6. See, *Election to Members of the Constituent Assembly* Act, 2007, Act No 2, 22 June, 2007.
7. *n.4.*
8. *n.6*: 16-17.
9. *n.6*: 34-38.

4

Formation of The Constituent Assembly

This chapter is devoted to an in-depth discussion of the issues raised by different political parties as a part of their campaign for the elections to the Constituent Assembly, their performance in the elections and the structure of the Constituent Assembly that has emerged after the elections.

Elections for 575 seats of the 601 member Constituent Assembly took place on 10 April 2008 almost a year after the first declaration of date for the elections. As pointed out earlier, dual electoral system was adopted for the Constituent Assembly elections. 240 seats were allocated for First Past The Post System (FPTP) and 335 seats for the Proportional Representation System (PRS). 26 members were to be nominated by the council of ministers from different walks of the Nepalese civil society.

It may be pointed out here that the importance of the elections of the Constituent Assembly lies in the fact that the Constituent Assembly would be proved as the corner stone of the institutionalization of peace process and the restructuring of the state in Nepal. It is a well known fact that the postponement of the elections of the Constituent Assembly for twice in June and November 2007 had aroused lot of controversies. Doubts were raised whether the political parties and political groups in Nepal were really interested in peace and stability? The postponement of the elections disturbed the Maoists particularly, who had given-up the insurgency and joined the mainstream politics, but were highly concerned about realization of their political goals through a democratic process. Therefore, the Constituent Assembly elections were a key moment towards the peace process.

Political Parties and Candidates

It has been made clear earlier that any party willing to participate in the Constituent Assembly elections required to register with the Election Commission. The Election Commission declared 14 January 2008 as the deadline for the registration of the political parties. Those political parties that were already registered with the Election Commission did not require a fresh registration. There were altogether 74 political parties registered with the Election Commission.

The political parties had to fulfill a dual task as far as the issue of nomination of the candidates was concerned. They had to nominate candidates for the First Past The Post System, and than also submit a closed list of candidates for the Proportional Representation System.

For the 240 seats of the Constituent Assembly under FPTP system 55 political parties nominated their candidates. The Communist Party of Nepal (Maoists) and the Nepali Congress were the only two political parties which nominated candidates for all the 240 seats. The UML was at third place with 339 seats. The other major political parties were: Rashtriya Prajatantra Party 232 candidates, Rashtriya Prajatantra Party (Nepal) 204, Jan Morcha Nepal 203, Rashtriya Janshakti Party 198, Communist Party of Nepal (Unified) 136, etc. Nepal Samyawadi Dal and Nepal Dalit Shramik Morcha had nominated only one candidate each in the elections. There were at least 17 political parties which had placed less than 10 candidates in the elections. It explains that perhaps these political parties had put its candidates in the elections just to ensure their existence as a political party. There were 816 independent candidates in the electoral fray out of which 42 were females and 774 males. There were altogether 3946 candidates.

For the Proportional Representation System out of 335 seats the Communist Party of Nepal had submitted a list of 333 candidates, the Communist Party of Nepal (UML) 332 candidates and Nepali Congress 329 candidates. Rashtriya Janmorcha also submitted a list of 333 candidates followed by Communist Party of Nepal (United) 328, Jan Morcha Prajatantra Party (Nepal) 221, etc. There were 19 political parties having submitted a list of less than 100 candidates and another 19 political parties having submitted a list of less than 50 candidates. There were altogether 5701 candidates under this system.

The political parties registered with the Election Commission and the list of candidates and tickets distributed by them for both PR and FPTP system underlined certain significant features:

1. Most of the political parties were towards the margin and they just in order to maintain their identity had nominated candidates and had given list of candidates. There were less than half a dozen major political parties, three of them being prominent as the Nepali Congress, (CPN (M) and CPN (UML).
2. There was larger number of political parties from the Tarai region. Apart from Nepal Sadbhawana Party (Anandi Devi) and Sadbhawana Party a number of other political parties had come up such as: Madheshi People's Rights Forum, Tarai Madheshi Loktantrik Party, Chure Bhawar Rastriya Ekta Party, etc. In fact, in the context of the autonomy movement in the Tarai in the recent past lot of political mobilization had taken place and new political organizations had come up. Earlier to that the Maoist movement had largely contributed to the radicalist political mobilization in the Tarai region.
3. Similarly, there seems larger representation of political parties belonging to ethnic groups, dalits, etc. The Mongol National Organization, Tamsaling Nepal Rastriya Dal, Nepal Sukumbasi Party, Nepal Dalit Shramik Morcha, Dalit Janjati Party, etc clearly shows the political mobilization of the ethnic groups and depressed communities of the Nepali society.
4. Most of the political parties decided to contest for the seats in the Constituent Assembly individually and no major political alignments were seen. The major political parties decided to take part in the elections independently. The Seven Party Alliance was there but the constituent political parties placed their candidates in the elections independently.

However, there were some exceptions to this. The Rashtriya Prajatantra Party, Rashtriya Prajatantra Nepal Party sought to form a front of the pro – monarchy or royalist political parties. Another alliance called Samyukta Samabeshi Morcha was also formed before the elections.

Party Manifestos and Programme

Most of the political parties came out with their election manifestos particularly dwelling up on the contemporary political issues in Nepal and their perception of the future political scenario of the country.

The Nepali Congress Party in its appeal to the voters stated that, "National Unity, pluralist democracy and maintenance of durable peace have been the agenda of Nepali Congress for a long time and they are our core agenda even to day. Institutionalization of democracy is the principal goal of NC; it has always been the guiding force in our decade's long struggle against autocracy. NC considers the formation of a Federal Democratic Republican State by using the mechanism of CA and by uniting all political forces of the country is its primary responsibility. The Congress party is committed to making constitution through its representatives elected in the CA while remaining true to the commitments as they are expressed in this manifesto".[1]

The Nepali Congress Party lodged the importance of Constituent Assembly in framing a democratic constitution. The party saw Constituent Assembly as a means to establish constitutional supremacy and rule of law and an opportunity to change the present centralized unitary state into a federal democratic structure.

It stated that the main agenda of the party in the Constituent Assembly elections was to save the country from right – wing monarchical extremism and the quagmire of militaristic violence championed by the Maoists. It was said, "We in NC want to create a peaceful, prosperous and democratic Nepal by ending the monarchy on the one hand and by facilitating a democratic transformation of the extremist left on the other".[2] The party raised a number of issues such as federal democracy, inclusive democracy, peace, equality and prosperity, community participation in development, cooperative movement, encouragement to investment and trade, employment and income generation, industrialization, water resources development, promotion of national unity and the strengthening of multi party democracy.

On the platform of international relations the Nepali Congress party envisaged main focus of its foreign policy on the protection of Nepal's sovereignty and promotion of independent identity and national interest in the international community so that it could contribute to international peace, goodwill and progress. It pledged support to UN charter, panchsheel and non – alignment. It said, "relations with our immediate neighbours, India and China, will be maintained according to widely accepted international norms and executed on a realist and pragmatic basis."

The Communist Party of Nepal (Maoist) strongly adhered to the Marxism – Leninism – Maoism as its guiding principle and communism as its goal. The party is committed to establish a democratic system adhering to people's sovereignty, justice and equality. In its manifesto the party accorded top priority to democracy, nationalism, federalism and economic transformation of the country. The party proposed 11 autonomous federal states and two other sub-states within them on the basis of ethnic composition, geography, linguistic base and economic viability. Seti-Mahakali and Bheri Karnali autonomous states are based on geography, Magrant, Tharuwan, Tamuwan, Newa, Tamsaling, Kirant, Limbuwan, Kochila, Madheshi on ethnicity and sub-states within Madheshi-Mithila, Bhojpura and Abadh based on language. The Maoists also reiterated that every autonomous state will have the right to self – determination. It was, however, stated that, "The right to self – determination will not lead the nation towards fragmentation rather it will keep the nation united by guaranteeing the rights of all castes and regions".[4]

The Maoist economic policy laid emphasis on tiller's right to land and socialist economy. It states that Nepal will reach to the level of highly developed states in 40 years. It also emphasized that Nepal's current per capita income of US $ 270 will be raised to US $ 3000 in next 10 years. Similarly the CPN (M) manifesto stated that Nepal will generate 10000 megawatt electricity in the next 10 years. It also promised to make drinking water available to the entire population of Nepal within a five years period. The party also stated that the illiteracy will be eradicated in five years time and that the health services will be made available to every person in Nepal.[5]

The Maoists also proposed formation of a national army by combining both the present army of Nepal and the people's liberation army belonging to the Maoists since the time of insurgency. The manifesto stated that "A national army will be formed by democratizing Nepali army and professionalizing people's liberation army". The Maoists also stressed upon raising employment opportunities in the country so that employment is ensured to all.

The Maoist leaders claimed that the party manifesto was a reflection of the ideas and goals envisaged by them during the decade long people's war.

The CPN (UML) is a party that traces its roots to the establishment of the Communist Party of Nepal on 22 April 1949. The party played an important role in the 1990 democratic movement and came to power in 1994-95. The party believes in the ideology of Marxism and Leninism but it has the image of a moderate party. It has been an important constituent of the Seven Party Alliance.

The party manifesto proposed for the election of the president by the elected parliament. It proposed that all administrative powers be given in the hands of the Prime Minister and the President would be the nominal head. Its manifesto also proposed for a bicameral legislative body at the centre and a unicameral legislature at each state under the new federal system. Thus the party supported a federal system for Nepal. The UML General Secretary said, "We have forwarded the principle of developing the federal structure on the basis of ethnic, culture and geographical distinctiveness. The party, however, did not give the number of states that it would propose. It was said that the states would be decided later by a state restructuring commission.

At the economic front party laid emphasis on the development of the public, private and cooperative sectors as the pillars of the Nepalese economy.

Madheshi People's Rights Forum of Nepal first came into existence in 1997 as a non – governmental organization called Janadhikar Forum. In early 2007 it was registered as a political party under the leadership of Upendra Yadav. The party participated in the Tarai uprising.

It is a region based party looking after the interest of the people of Tarai and wishes to ensure rights and representation of the Madheshis. The party has believed in social democracy.

The party advocated for a single autonomous Madheshi state with the right to self – determination. It also proposed for a directly elected executive president to act as head of state.

Tarai Madheshi Loktantrik party emerged in January 2008 in the context of the Tarai agitation. The party had submitted an 11 point demand charter to Koirala government with a deadline of 18 January 2008. It included immediate declaration of Nepal as a federal republic, granting of autonomy to a single Madheshi province and proportional representation to all ethnic communities in state structure, including the army. The aprty believed in democratic socialism and serving the interest of the Madheshis has been its main moto.

It also supported a ceremonial president as head of the state. It gave the slogan of 'Ek Madhesh Ek Pradesh' (One Madheshi One State).

The Communist Party of Nepal (United) pleaded for a ceremonial head of the state and the Prime Minister as the chief executive. **Chure Bhawar Rashtriya Ekta Party** formed in 2007 called for autonomy to the Chure Bhawar region. The party opined that the fate of monarchy and the question of secular or Hindu state be decided through referendum. It also sated that the federal units be decided on the basis of geography and resource distribution not ethnicity.

Nepal Loktantrik Samajbadi Dal proposed for a bicameral legislature, one chamber as the House of Representatives and another as the House of Ethnic Representative. The first would choose the Prime Minister who will be the executive head and the second would choose the president who would serve as the ceremonial head of the state. The party proposed nine federal units based on history, geography, population and language.

Dalit Janjati Party demanded 13 per cent reservation for dalits in all government jobs. It also supported the ceremonial head of state and federal units based on ethnic lines.

The Federal Democratic National Forum an umbrella organization of parties representing Tharu, Rai, Limbu, Tamang communities supported completely proportional elections for CA; 13 federal units with right to self – determination and abolition of monarchy. **Nepal Workers and Peasants Party** proposed a directly elected executive president as head of the state who will also head of the army. The party also proposed turning the existing zones into provincial boundaries.

The Communist Party of Nepal (Unified) called for immediate abolition of monarchy through a motion in the Legislature – Parliament and federalism based an ethnicity or geography. **Rashtriya Janmorcha** on the other hand was the only left party opposed to federalism as it could lead to disintegration of the country.

Sadbhawana Party propsed an indirectly elected president and a powerful Prime Minister. It proposed three federal units for Nepal: Madheshi, Hills and Mountains.

Rashtriya Prajatantra Party a right – wing party of the former panchayat leaders proposed that the issues of monarchy and secularism should be directly decided by the sovereign people. The party emphasized a federal system in place of unitary state. The **Rashtriya Prajatanta Party Nepal**, a splinter group of RPP on the other hand supported a ceremonial monarchy as head of the state. It also pleaded that the issue of federalism be decided on the basis of a broad national consensus.

The other political parties also raised the similar issues. The generally agreed issues by most of the political parties were

: The westminister model of governance – a ceremonial head of the state and a powerful head of the government.

: Abolition of monarchy and republican state.

: Federalism in place of unitary state.

: Secular State.

: Inclusive democracy.

: Balanced foreign policy based on equal relationship with its two neighbours.

: Economic reforms.

Republican state, inclusive democracy and federalism were the issues which most of the political parties talked about and there was a consensus barring a few political parties that wanted the issue of monarchy to be left for the people to decide upon.

Polling Arrangements

The polling for 240 seats of the Constituent Assembly on the basis of the First Past The Post System took place on 10 April 2008 at 20,000 polling stations all over the country. Repolling took place in 98 polling stations of 21 constituencies in 12 districts.

A large number of internal and international observers were nominated for the elections. In fact, the reports indicated that this election had the highest number of observers. There were 60,000 internal and 800 international observers nominated. Some of the prominent agencies which appointed their observers were the UN, the European Union, The Carter Centre, The Asian Network for Free Elections, the Japanese Observer Mission, etc.

UN Role in the Elections

The United Nations played a significant role in the successful completion of the elections to the Constituent Assembly. In fact, the UN had been active in Nepal since the beginning of the peace process and had played a vital role in the management of the Maoist arms and their combatants. The Nepalese government had requested for the presence of the UN representatives in the CA elections.

The UN Mission (UNMIN) was established in Nepal by the UN Security Council under its resolution 1740 (2007) at the request of the Nepalese government. It was stated that apart from its support in the peace process the mission will also help in conducting the Constituent Assembly elections and creating a free and fair atmosphere for the elections. It was expected that the UN Mission would help the Nepal Election Commission and work in close cooperation with the UN agencies and the UNHCHR Mission in Nepal.

The UN Mission helped in the elections of the Constituent Assembly in following ways.

1. The UNMIN Electoral Assistance Office worked together with the Election Commission of Nepal for more than a year in Kathmandu and all regions. It provided assistance and legal advice in areas such as the legal framework, voter education, media monitoring and logistics. The election experts from the UN Volunteer Programme were deployed as district electoral advisors in all the 75 districts of the country towards the last phase of the elections. These advisers were supposed to support the work of the District Electoral Officers of the Election Commission of Nepal.
2. The United Nations itself did not observe the elections but a team called Electoral Expert Monitoring Team consisting of renowned electoral experts was constituted by the UN Secretary General. The team was to advise the UNMIN as well as Nepal Election Commission and submit a report to the Secretary General finally.
3. UNDP supported the Election Commission of Nepal in providing coordinated information and assistance to election observers.
4. The UN agencies and the UNHCHR deployed teams on the day of voting in nearly 45 districts to help preparing an atmosphere of confidence among voters, so that peaceful voting could take place.

5. UNMIN officials monitored Nepali army and the Maoist combatants to remain in their cantonments or barracks and only go out to cast their votes. On Election Day monitors were posted in all 28 cantonments and army locations.

Voting Turnout

The total voters in the April 2008 CA elections were 17.6 million. It indicated an increase of voters in comparison to the last election held in 1999. The exact voters for this election were 17611832.

The voting turnout was 65.15 per cent in 1991 elections of the parliament; 61.86 per cent in 1994 and 65.79 per cent in 1999 general election.[3] Total votes polled were 11146540. Out of these votes 407462 votes were rejected. Thus the valid votes were 10739078. The voting percentage remained 63.29 and the percentage of rejected votes was 3.66. It gives an impression that the voting percentage was lower in the Constituent Assembly elections in comparison to the earlier general elections.

Table No – 1

Voters and Voting Trends

S.No.	*Categories*	*Total*
1.	Total Voters	17611832
2.	Total Votes Polled	11146540
3.	Invalid Votes	407462
4.	Valid Votes	10739078
5.	Voting Percentage	63.29
6.	Invalid Vote Percentage	3.66

Partywise Position under FPTPS

As pointed out earlier, 240 seats were fixed out of a total seats of 601 for election under the First Past The Post System, distributed over 75 districts of the country. 54 Political parties nominated their candidates for these seats. Interestingly only 9 political parties could register their victory. It means that 45 political parties could not win even a single seat. Thus the percentage of unrepresented political parties being 83.3. Thus only 16.7 per cent political parties got representation in the CA through FPTP system. Some of the prominent political parties which could not secure a single seat were the Communist Party of Nepal (UML), the Rashtriya Prajatantra Party, etc.

The Communist Party of Nepal (Maoist) emerged as the largest party with 120 seats. Thus the party secured 50 per cent of the total seats. There were expectations that the CPN (M) would have a better performance in the elections looking back to its immediate past. In fact it was CPN (M) which had brought the country to this stage. The credit of elections to the CA goes to Maoists. The strategy of Maoists to give up the insurgency and move on democratic path for the realization of its political goals also proved to be fruitful in terms of their participation in the elections. The commitment of the party for the abolition of monarchy and declaring Nepal a republican sate, restructuring of state, inclusive democracy, federal structure and autonomy, etc attracted different sections of the society particularly the ethnic and the marginalized communities. The Maoists could mobilize support from diverse sections of the society, women, youth, peasants, labourers, tribals, dalits, etc. The Maoists have their strong bases, particularly in the mid – western Nepal. The emergence of CPN (Maoist) as the largest party in the elections is also significant keeping in view the facts that:

: The party and its leaders hardly had any experience either as a ruling party or opposition party, compared to the Nepali Congress, UML, National Democratic Party or CPN (ML), etc.

: The Maoists had been involved in a protracted war fighting against the state for over a decade.

: They had been declared terrorists and the Royal Nepal Army had been deployed to contain them by force.

: A large number of people, particularly in the countryside had become victims of the Maoist atrocities.

Than in mid 2006 the Maoists gave up protracted guerrilla war and joined hands with Seven Party Alliance for a peaceful and democratic political transition. So, the Maoists formed a different category of political groups in Nepal. It seems that the people wanted a change: the restructuring of society and state. They laid their hopes on the Maoists who had indeed exhibited a strong commitment to restructuring of state and society.

The Nepali Congress, the doyan of democratic movement in Nepal, on the other hand, exhibited a poor performance by bagging only 37 seats. The party obtained 15.5 per cent of the total seats. An Almost similar fate was that of the CPN (UML) a party that had been claiming as a major communist force in the country in the past. The party secured only 33 seats with its percentage of seats being 13.7. Both the parties are considered to be the largest having wide social base. But the problem with these political parties was that they could not take a clear stand on the issues that had been coming up on the Nepalese political scene for last some years. The people of Nepal wanted a change and these parties were not forthright on the issue of change. For instance on the question of monarchy vis-à-vis republican state, the Nepali Congress maintained an ambiguous position at the initial stage. The problem with the UML was that the party had been considering itself as the main proponent of the communist ideology in Nepal. But they were over taken by the Maoists. So they too were hesistent in lending their allout support to the issues raised by the Maoists.

It is true that the CPN (Maoist) too failed in seeking a majority. But it is also a fact that it was not as established a political party as the Nepali Congress or the UML.

In comparison to the Nepali Congress and the UML Madheshi Janadhikar Forum registered a much impressive performance. A party that had made a very recent debut did quite well by bagging 30 seats – a share of 12.6 per cent. The Madheshi Janadhikar Forum being a regional party secured all its seats from the Tarai region. In fact, the party has been a strong proponent of regional autonomy and participated in the Tarai agitation. The significant point that needs to be mentioned here is that the Madheshi Janadhikar Forum has emerged as the fourth largest party in the Constituent Assembly. Another party from Tarai: Tarai Madheshi Loktantrik Party secured 9 seats its percentage being 3.7. It also emerged as a political party in the context of 2007 Tarai agitation. The Sadbhawana Party representing Tarai for quite some time go shifted to background in comparison to these two parties with only 4 seats. Nevertheless, it can be said that it was for the first time that the Tarai region got some representation in the representative institutions of the country.

Nepal Majdoor Kishan Paty and its undisputed leader Narainman Bijukche once again established that Bhaktpur is its strong hold. It won on both seats of Bhaktpur. One would like to remind here that the party has been representing these two constituencies since long. Bhaktpur is an important segment of the Kathmandu valley and here the literacy rate is near 90 per cent much above to national average. But one has also to bear in mind that the party could not won a single seat elsewhere.

The other parties too had a marginal representation such as Janmorcha Nepal 2 and Rashtriya Janmorcha 1. The independent candidates had a decimal performance as out of 800 independent candidates only 2 could reach to the Constituent Assembly.

Table No – 2

Seats Obtained by Political Parties in CA (FPTP)

S. No.	*Political Parties*	*Seats Owned*	*Percentage*
1.	Communist Party of Nepal (Maoist)	120	50.0
2.	Nepali Congress	37	15.5
3.	Communist Party of Nepal (UML)	33	13.7
4.	Madheshi Janadhikar Forum	30	12.6
5.	Tarai Madheshi Loktantrik Party	9	3.7
6.	Sadbhawana Party	4	1.7
7.	Nepal Majdoor Kishan Party	2	0.8
8.	Janmorcha Nepal	2	0.8
9.	Rashtriya Janmorcha	1	0.4
10.	Independents	2	0.8
Total		**240**	**100.0**

Party Performance According to Geographic Regions

The distribution of seats according to three geographic regions of the country was mountains 22, hills 102 and Tarai 116. The distribution of seats among the political parties in three geographic regions reveals certain interesting features. In the mountains it was CPN (Maoist) which proved its dominant position. It baged 16 out of 22 seats, thus its share being 72.7 per cent. The CPN (UML) secured 4 seats while Nepali Congress could win on two seats only.

In the hill areas the three major political parties the CPN (Maoist), Nepali Congress and CPN (UML) performed almost equally. CPN (M) received 51.6 per cent of its total seats from the hills, Nepali Congress 51.4 and CPN (UML) 54.6 per cent. The other parties which recorded their lone victory in the hills were Nepal Majdoor Kishan Party (2) and Rashtriya Janmorcha (1).

In the Tarai region the Nepali Congress performed better in comparison to the CPN (M) and CPN (UML). The Tarai region has been viewed as a traditional strong hold of the Nepali Congress. But in the Constituent Assembly elections what appears to be detrimental to the Nepali Congress and CPN (M) to some extent, is the emergence of regional parties in the context of the autonomy movement in Tarai. Madheshi Janadhikar Forum (30) and Tarai Madheshi Loktantrik Party (9) together bagged 39 seats from Tarai. Interestingly, these parties had been formed during 2007-2008 only. Sadbhawana Party got 4 stats, Janmorcha Nepal 2 seats and independents won on two seats of Tarai. Thus all together 47 seats (40.5 percent) went to non-Nepali and non CPN (M) – CPN (UML) parties. This trend appears to be quite significant for three reasons:

1. Rise of regional parties.
2. Increased representation of Madheshis in national political institutions.
3. Significance of the question of regional autonomy.

On contrary, in comparison to the regional parties, the ethnicity based parties had a decimal performance in the Constituent Assembly elections. Mongol National organization a fairly older organization in comparison to the recently organized Tarai parties, could not register victory on a single seat. Similar was the case with other ethnic based parties such as Tamsaling Nepal National Party, Nepal Sukumbasi Party, etc. Similar was the story of dalit parties like Nepal Dalit Shramik Morcha and Dalit Janjati Party.

Table No – 3

Regional Distribution of Seats among Political Parties

(Direct Elections)

S.No.	*Parties / Regions*	*Mountain %*	*Hills %*	*Tarai %*	*Total*
1.	Communist Party of Nepal (Maoist)	16 13.4	62 51.6	42 35.0	120
2.	Nepali Congress	02 5.4	19	16	37
3.	Communist Party of Nepal (UML)	04 12.1	18	11 33.0	33
4.	Madheshi Janadhikar Forum	---		30	30
5.	Tarai Madheshi Loktantrik Party	---		9	9
6.	Sadbhawana Party	---		4	4

7.	Nepal Majdur Kishan Party	---	2		2
8.	Janmorcha Nepal			2	2
9.	Rashtriya Jan Morcha			1	1
10.	Independents			2	2
Total		**22**	**102**	**116**	**240**

Party Positions in Development Regions

In the five development regions of the country, Central Development Region was allocated the highest number of seats (81) followed by Eastern Development Region (50). Far Western Development Region had the lowest number of seats (21). The CPN (M) exhibited a good hold in Mid Western and Far Western Development Regions, particularly in Mid Western Region where it bagged 27 out of a total of 33 seats. The Nepali Congress had a comparatively better position in the Central Development Region. The CPN (UML) performed almost equally in Central Development Region, Eastern Development Region and Western Development Region.

The regional parties were by and large concentrated in Central and Eastern Development Regions.

In terms of distribution of seats among parties according to administrative zones certain revealing trends can be seen. In Rapti and Karnali zones all the thirteen seats were bagged by the Maoists. The Nepali Congress did well in Lumbini zone where it could secure all seats, followed by Bagmati, 7 seats. The UML seats were equally distributed in different zones except Mahakali, Karnali, Rapti and Sagarmatha zones where it could not secure a single seat. The Nepali Congress also failed in securing any seat in Karnali, Rapti and Gandaki zones. Thus, CPN (M) was the only party which had made its presence felt in all the 14 administrative zones of the country. It is indeed a significant development because it reflects upon the bases of the party. Far a political party aspiring to become a national party not only it is significant how much seats it gains but the equally important fact is how much area it has covered. In this context one may say that CPN (M) has emerged as the only party having a nationwide coverage.

Table No – 4

Positions of Political Parties in CA According to Development Regions

S.No.	Party/ DR	DR	CPN (M)	NC	UML	MJF	TMLP	SP	UMKP	JM	RJM	IND
1.	EDR	56 (23.3)	23 (19.2)	7 (18.9)	8 24.2	16 53.3	--	1 25.0				1 50.0
2.	CDR	81 (33.7)	37 (30.8)	16 (43.2)	8 24.2	7 23.3	5 55.5	3 75.0	2 100.0			1 50.0
3.	UDR	49 (20.4)	18 (15.0)	10 (27.0)	11 33.4	5 16.7	4 44.5			1 100.0	1	
4.	MWDR	33 (13.8)	27 (22.5)	1 (2.7)	3 9.1	2 6.7						
5.	FWDR	21 (8-8)	15 (12.5)	3 (8.2)	3 9.1							
Total		240 100.0	120 100.0	37 100.0	33	30	9	4	2	1	1	2 100.0

Table No – 5

Distribution of Seats Among Political Parties According to Administrative Zones

S. No.	*Ad. Zones*	*Total Const.*	*CPN (M)*	*NC*	*UML*	*MJM*	*TMLP*	*SP*	*NMKP*	*JM*	*RJM*	*IND*
1.	Mahakali	8	6	2								
2.	Seti	13	9	1	3							
3.	Karnali	5	5									
4.	Bheri	15	9	1	3	2						
5.	Rapti	13	13									
6.	Dhaulagiri	7	2	2	2						1	
7.	Lumbini	32	8	9	6	5	4					
8.	Gandaki	10	8		2							
9.	Narayani	26	11	5	3	2	2	1		1		1
10.	Bagmati	29	19	7	1				2			
11.	Janakpur	26	7	3	5	5	3	2		1		
12.	Sagarmatha	20	8	1		9		1	1			1
13.	Koshi	21	10	2	3	7						
14.	Mechi	14	5	4	5							
	Total	240	120	37	33	30	9	4	2	2	1	2

Table No – 6

District Wise Distribution of Seats Among Political Parties

S. No.	Districts/ Political Parties	Const.	1 CPN (M)	2 NC	3 UML	4 MJM	5 TMLP	6 SP	7 NMKP	8 JM	9 RJM	10 IND
1.	Taplejung	2		1	1							
2.	Panchthar	2		1	1							
3.	Ilam	3		1	2							
4.	Jhapa	7	5	1	1							
5.	Sankhuwasabha	2	1		1							
6.	Teharthum	1		1								
7.	Bhojpur	2	2									
8.	Dhankuta	2	2									
9.	Morang	9	4	1		4						
10.	Sunsari	6	1		2	3						
11.	Solu Khumbu	1	1									
12.	Khotang	2	2									
13.	Okhaldhunga	2	2									
14.	Udaypur	3	2	1								
15.	Saptari	6				5		1				1

16.	Sirha	6	1			5						
17.	Dolakha	2	2									
18.	Rameechap	2	2									
19.	Sindhuli	3	2		1							
20.	Dhanusha	7	1	3	2	1						
21.	Mahottari	6				3	2			1		
22.	Sarlahi	6		2	1	1	2					
23.	Rasuwa	1	1									
24.	Dhading	3	3									
25.	Nuwakot	3	2	1								
26.	Kathmandu	10	4	6								
27.	Bhaktapur	2							2			
28.	Lalitput	3	3									
29.	Kavre	4	3		1							
30.	Sindhupalan-chok	3	3									
31.	Makwanpur	4	4									
32.	Rauthat	6	2	2			1					1
33.	Bara	6	2	1		1	1	1				
34.	Parsa	5	4	3	1	1						
35.	Chitwan	5	3		1					1		
36.	Gorkha	3	3									

37.	Manang	1	1									
38.	Lamjung	2	1		1							
39.	Kaski	4	3		1							
40.	Tanahu	3	1	1	1							
41.	Syangja	3		2	1							
42.	Gulmi	3	2		1							
43.	Palpa	3	1		2							
44.	Arghakhanchi	2	1	1								
45.	Nawalparasi	6	2	2		1	1					
46.	Rupandehi	7	1	1	2	3						
47.	Kapilbastu	5		1		1	3					
48.	Mustang	1			1							
49.	Myanagdi	1	1									
50.	Baglung	3		1	1						1	
51.	Parbat	2	1	1								
52.	Rukum	2	2									
53.	Rolpa	2	2									
54.	Pyuthan	2	2									
55.	Salyan	2	2									
56.	Dang	5	5									
57.	Dolpa	1	1									
58.	Mugu	1	1									

59.	Jumla	1	1									
60.	Kalikot	1	1									
61.	Humla	1	1									
62.	Jajarkot	1	2									
63.	Dailekh	2		1	1							
64.	Surkhet	3	1		2							
65.	Banke	4	2			2						
66.	Bardiya	4	4									
67.	Bajura	1		1								
68.	Achham	2	1		1							
69.	Bajhang	2	1		1							
70.	Doti	2	1		1							
71.	Kailali	6	6									
72.	Darchula	1	1									
73.	Baitadi	2	2									
74.	Dadeldhura	1		1								
75.	Kanchanpur	4	3	1								

This can be further substantiated on the basis of district wise performance of the political parties. The CPN (M) registered its presence by winning at least one seat in 64 of 75 districts. Thus it could not win any seat in 11 districts. The Nepali Congress on the other hand could not open its account in 50 of 75 districts. Thus it won in 25 districts only. It clearly shows that the base of the Nepali Congress has considerably narrowed down. The CPN (UML) also faced a similar situation as it could not win a single seat in 48 districts.

The CPN (M) completely dominated in 31 districts, while the Nepal Congress dominated in 3 districts, UML in one district and Nepal Majdur Kishan Party also in one district.

Table No – 7

CPN (Maosits) Dominated Districts (% Basis)

S.No.	District	S.No.	District
1.	Bhojpur	17.	Rolpa
2.	Dhankuta	18.	Pyuthan
3.	Khotang	19.	Salyan
4.	Okhaldunga	20.	Dang
5.	Dailakha	21	Dolpa
6.	Rameechap	22.	Mugu
7.	Solukhumbu	23.	Jumla
8.	Rasuwa	24.	Kalikot
9.	Dhading	25.	Humla
10.	Lalitpur	26.	Jajarkot
11.	Sindhupalchock	28.	Bardiya
12.	Makwanpur	29.	Kailali
13.	Gorkha	30.	Darchula
14.	Manang	31.	Betadi
15.	Mynagdi		
16.	Rukum		

Talbe No – 8

Nepali Congress Dominated Districts

S.No.	District
1.	Teharthum
2.	Bajura
3.	Dadeldhura

UML Dominated Districts

S.No.	District
1.	Mustang

NMKP Dominated Districts

S.No.	District
1.	Bhaktapur

The Maoist Heartland

The Mid Western Development Region of Nepal has once again emerged as the heartland of the Maoists. The Constituent Assembly elections have proved it that the hold of the CPN (Maoist) in this region can not be challenged. The Maoists won in all the 16 seats in Dolpa, Pyuthan, Rolpa, Rukum, Salyan, Dang and Jajarkot districts. These districts form the nucleus from where the Maoist insurgency began and it emerged as the headquarters of the Maoist rebellion. The Maoist leaders had started their activities in this region after 1991 general elections and more intensively after 1994 mid–term elections. But the mid western hills had been nurtured in the form of a communist hub by hardcore communist leaders like Mohan Bikram Singh since early. He worked here nearly for 24 years. The Communist Party of Nepal had won a seat in the 1959 parliamentary elections from this region.

In Kathmandu on the other hand the Nepali Congress performed well. It bagged 6 of 10 seats the CPN (M) got 4 seats. In Lalitpur, however, all the three seats were won by the CPN (M) and two seats of Bhaktpur were won by Nepal Majdoor Kishan Party. The CPN (UML) could not won a single seat in Kathmandu valley.

Table No – 9

CPN (M) Performance in the Heartland of the Maoist Movement (MWDR)

S.No.	*Districts*	*Seats Allotted*	*Seats Woned by CPN (M)*
1.	Dolpa	1	1
2.	Peyuthan	2	2
3.	Rolpa	2	2
4.	Rukum	2	2
5.	Salyan	2	2
6.	Dang	5	5
7.	Jajarkot	2	2
	Total	16	16 100% seats captured by Maoists

Table No – 10

Constituency Wise Party Position in Kathmandu Valley

Kathmandu	*NC*	*UML*	*CPN (M)*	*Others*
Area 1	14318	6789	4837	
Area 2	8896	10218	13878	
Area 3	12989	8127	6289	
Area 4	11742	8814	8405	
Area 5	12886	8559	7779	
Area 6	7261	7678	8634	
Area 7	9693	7614	10489	
Area 8	11005	4402	4156	
Area 9	11686	4939	11628	
Area 10	12154	6335	23277	
Lalitpur				
Area 1	14011	8687	15325	
Area 2	15295	11300	16960	
Area 3	9700	10048	17789	
Bhaktapur				
Area 1	6479		9256	19972 (NMKP)
Area 2	10940	8745		18100 (NMKP)

Table No – 11

Party Position in Kathmandu Valley

S.No.	*Party*	*Seats Won*
1.	CPN (Maoist)	7
2.	Nepali Congress	6
3.	CPN – UML	0
4.	Nepal Majdoor Kishan Party	2

Table No – 12

Age Structure (FPTP)

S.No.	*Age Groups*	*Nos.*	*Percentage*
1.	25 – 35 Years	60	25.0
2.	36 – 45 Years	71	29.6
3.	46 – 55 Years	75	31.2
4.	56 – 65 Years	25	10.4
5.	66 – 75 Years	5	2.1
6.	75 Years & above		
7.	Not Stated	4	1.7
Total		**240**	**100.0**

Age Structure

The age structure of the representatives in the Constituent Assembly reveals that the majority of the elected persons belong to younger age group of 25 to 45 years of age (54.6 %). 31.2 percent belonged to middle age group of 46 – 55 years. Only 10.4 percent were in the higher age group of 50 -65 years and 2.1 percent above 66 years. This trend is important in the context of Nepal's quest for political transformation. It seems that the younger generation has been attracted to the issues of republican state, federalism, etc.

It may further be seen that most of the representatives in the category of 25 – 35 years of age belonged to the CPN (Maoist). Similarly the representative between 36 – 45 years also largely belonged to the CPN (Maoist). The majority of the Nepali Congress and CPN (UML) representatives belonged to middle age between 46 – 55 years. It clearly shows that the younger people have a liking towards the CPN (Maoist).

Table No – 13

Age Groups According to Political Parties

S. No.	*Name of the Party*	*Age Group*						
		25-35	*36-45*	*46-55*	*56-65*	*66-75*	*75 & above*	*NS*
1.	Nepali Congress	2	5	16	10	4		
2.	CPN (UML)		12	18	3			
3.	CPN (Maoist)	48	38	25	6			3
4.	MJF	8	6	10	5			1
5.	Independent	1	1	0				
6.	Rashtriya Janmorcha		1					
7.	Sadbhawana Party	1	2	1				
8.	NWPP		1			1		
9.	Janmorcha Nepal		1	1				
10.	TMLP		4	4	1			
		60	71	75	25	5		

Gender Profile

The issue of appropriate gender representation is also significant in the context of inclusive democracy. In Nepal women have been meagerly represented in the political and administrative institutions. It was expected in the Constituent Assembly elections that women would receive more attention in comparison to the earlier elections for two reasons: firstly, the issue of empowerment of women has gradually come up in Nepal during the last few years. Secondly, the Maoist insurgency had mobilized women and aroused their aspirations for equitable representation in politico – administrative structures.

Table No – 14

Gender Profile of Direct Elected Members of CA

S.No.	Gender	Seats Occupied	Percentage
1.	Female	30	12.5
2.	Male	210	87.5
Total		**240**	**100.0**

In the Constituent Assembly elections out of 54 political parties 39 gave tickets to women candidates as well, although 14 of them took up only one to two women candidates. The CPN (Maoist) distributed 21.8 per cent of its total seats to women candidates, while the Nepali Congress allotted only 12.1 per cent seats to women candidates. The CPN (UML) also allotted 12.7 per cent seats to women. It shows that the CPN (Maoist) proved to be more progressive in taking up the issue of gender representation.

The performance of women was, however, not much impressive in the Constituent Assembly elections as only 30 (12.5 %) women recorded their victory. Interestingly, 24 (8.0%) women representatives belonged to CPN (Maoist). Others were two Nepali Congress, two Madheshi People's Rights Forum, One UML and One Tarai Madheshi Loktantrik Party.

One may say that 12.5 per cent is not a significant share but taking into consideration the Nepalese conditions the trend is encouraging.

Table No – 15

Party-wise Gender Representation

S.No.	Party Name	Candidate		Total	Elected		
		Female	Male		Female	Male	Total
1.	Communist Party of Nepal (Maoist)	43	197	240	24	96	120
2.	Nepali Congress	26	214	240	2	35	37
3.	Communist Party of Nepal (UML)	27	212	239	1	32	33
4.	Madheshi People's Rights Forum,	3	100	103	2	27	29
5.	Tarai Madheshi Loktantrik Party	4	90	94	1	8	9
6.	Sadhvawana Party	4	83	87	0	4	4
7.	Janamorcha Nepal	28	175	203	0	2	2
8.	Nepal Workers and Peasants Party	27	71	98	0	2	2
9.	Independents	42	774	816	0	2	2
10.	Rastriya Janamorcha	15	107	122	0	1	1
11.	Rastriya Janshakti Party	14	184	198	0	0	0
12.	Rastriya Prajatantra Party	22	210	232	0	0	0

13.	Samajwadi Prajatantrik Janata Party, Nepal	7	43	50	0	0	0
14.	Nepal Rastriya Bikas Party	0	13	13	0	0	0
15.	Socialist Party of Nepal	0	5	5	0	0	0
16.	Rastriya Janamukti Party	8	76	84	0	0	0
17.	Rastriya Prajatantra Party Nepal	8	196	204	0	0	0
18.	Communist Party of Nepal (Unified)	10	126	136	0	0	0
19.	C.ommunist Party of Nepal (M.L.)	11	105	116	0	0	0
20.	Rastriya Janata Dal	0	8	8	0	0	0
21.	Communist Party of Nepal (United)	6	49	55	0	0	0
22.	Nepal Samata Party	2	12	14	0	0	0
23.	Dalit Janajati Party	1	49	50	0	0	0
24.	Nepal Sadhvawana Party (Anandi Devi)	13	91	104	0	0	0
25.	Communist Party of Nepal (United Marxist)	5	43	48	0	0	0
26.	Communist Party of Nepal (Marxist)	1	7	8	0	0	0

27.	Hindu Democratic Party	0	4	4	0	0	0
28.	Nav Janawadi Morcha	1	14	15	0	0	0
29.	Nepal Rastriya Janakalyan Party	0	3	3	0	0	0
30.	Rastriya Bikas Party	0	21	21	0	0	0
31.	Muskan Sena Nepal Party	2	32	34	0	0	0
32.	League Nepal Shanti Ekata Party	0	10	10	0	0	0
33.	Nepal Janabhawana Party	0	2	2	0	0	0
34.	Nepal Shanti Kshetra Pari-shad	1	2	3	0	0	0
35.	Rastrawadi Yuwa Morcha	1	4	5	0	0	0
36.	Liberal Samajwadi Party	0	3	3	0	0	0
37.	Nepali Janata Dal	10	30	40	0	0	0
38.	Nepal Rastriya Lokatantrik Dal	1	1	2	0	0	0
39.	Rastrawadi Ekata Party	2	0	2	0	0	0
40.	Janamukti Party, Nepal	0	3	3	0	0	0
41.	Sa-Shakti Nepal	6	0	6	0	0	0
42.	Rastriya Janata Dal Nepal	0	17	17	0	0	0
43.	Shanti Party Nepal	4	8	12	0	0	0

44.	Nepal Janata Party	2	23	25	0	0	0
45.	Lok Kalyankari Janata Party Nepal	2	32	34	0	0	0
46.	Mongol National Organiza-tion	0	17	17	0	0	0
47.	Nepal Samyawadi Dal	0	1	1	0	0	0
48.	Federal Democratic Na-tional Forum	2	43	45	0	0	0
49.	Nepal Rastriya Party	1	5	6	0	0	0
50.	Nepal Lokatantrik Sama-jbadi Dal	0	11	11	0	0	0
51.	Nepal Sukumbasi Party (Loktantrik)	3	8	11	0	0	0
52.	Nepal Dalit Shramik Mor-cha	0	1	1	0	0	0
53.	Chure Bhawar Rastriya Ekata Party Nepal	1	21	22	0	0	0
54.	Tamsaling Nepal Rastriya Dal	3	19	22	0	0	0
55.	Nawanepal Prajatantrik Dal	0	2	2	0	0	0
	Total	**369**	**3577**	**3946**	**30**	**209**	**239**

Ethnic Representation in CA

The question of ethnic representation has equally been important in Nepal. There has been a strong discontent among ethnic groups regarding upper caste domination in representative bodies. The Mongolian groups have been resenting against Bahunwad. In a plural society a broad based political representation is necessary for the successful working of democracy. The Mongolian organizations had started demanding their adequate representation in political institutions as early as 1980. But it was only after 1990 that some change was visible in this regard. A greater ethnic mobilization took place during the Maoist insurgency in Nepal.

The ethnic composition of the CA members under FPTP system shows certain significant trends. The tribal communities have secured 33.3 per cent seats which is the highest representation of a particular group in CA. The once dominating Brahmins have gone down to second place with 24.6 per cent seats. Equally important is the fact that the Madheshis had got third place with 22.5 per cent. Chettris got 12.9 per cent seats.

Table No – 16

Ethnic Profile of Representatives (FPTP)

S. No.	*Ethnicity*	*Number*	*Percentage*
1.	Bahun	59	24.6
2.	Chettri	31	12.9
3.	Janjati	80	33.3
4.	Madheshii	54	22.5
5.	Dalit	07	2.9
6.	Unstated	09	3.8
Total		**240**	**100**

In terms of the party basis of ethnic groups it can be seen that majority of the Madheshii representatives belong to the Tarai based regional parties. Similarly, majority of the Janjati representatives belong to the CPN (Maoist) (65.0 per cent). In the case of Nepali Congress 56.7 per cent representatives belong to Brahmin – Chettri groups. The Brahmins alone form 35.1 percent of its total winning candidates.

Table No – 17

Party Wise Representation of Ethnic Groups

S. No.	*Parties*	*Ethnic Groups*						
		Bahun	*Chettri*	*Janjati*	*Madheshi*	*Dalit*	*Unstated*	*Total*
1.	CPN (M)	32	16	52	08	07	05	**120**
2.	NC	13	08	10	05		01	**37**
3.	UML	10	05	12	04		02	**33**
4.	MJF	02	01	03	24			**30**
5.	TMLP	01			07		01	**09**
6.	SP				04			**04**
7.	NMKP			02				**02**
8.	Jan Morcha	01		01				**02**
9.	Rashtriya Janmorcha		01					**01**
10.	Independents				02			**02**
	Total	**54**	**31**	**80**	**54**	**07**	**09**	**240**

Representation of Dalits

It is also a significant development that the Dalits have got representation in the Constituent Assembly. Seven Dalit candidates have been elected. It is not a significant number in the over all context but it is important in the sense that the earlier notions of Nepalese society and polity are undergoing a change.

It can be said that this change has occurred in the context of the political transformation taking place in Nepal and the role played by the CPN (Maoist) towards mobilization of marginalized social groups. It is interesting that seven dalit candidates have been elected for the Constituent Assembly and all the seven candidates belong to CPN (Maoist). Four other Dalit contestants which ranked second also belonged to the same party.

Representation Under Proportional Representation System

It has already been made clear that 335 seats of the Constituent Assembly were to be filled through proportional representation as per procedure discussed in earlier chapter.

Table No – 18

Dalit Candidates in Constituency Wise Top Three Position

S. No	*District*	*Const.*	*Candidate's Name*	*Party/ Independent*	*Gend*	*Total Votes*	*Remarks*
1.	Kalikot	1	Khadga Bahadur Bishwa-karma	Communist Party of Nepal (Maoist)	M	27629	Elected
2.	Kavrepalan chok	4	Tej Bahadur Mijar	Communist Party of Nepal (Maoist)	M	22076	Elected
3.	Banke	1	Tilak Pariyar	Communist Party of Nepal (Maoist)	M	16087	Elected
4.	Kaski	4	Durga Kumari B.K	Communist Party of Nepal (Maoist)	F	14866	Elected
5.	Morang	8	Gopi Bahadur Sarki (Ach-hami)	Communist Party of Nepal (Maoist)	M	14375	Elected
6.	Nawalparasi	3	Sita Devi Poudel	Communist Party of Nepal (Maoist)	F	13535	Elected

7.	Siraha	5	Mahendra Paswan	Communist Party of Nepal (Maoist)	M	12110	Elected
8.	Tanahu	2	Dambar Bahadur Bishwerkarma	Communist Party of Nepal (Maoist)	M	11050	Second Position
9	Nawalparasi	5	Raju Prasad Chamar Harijan	Communist Party of Nepal (Maoist)	M	10849	Second Position
10.	Arghakhanchi	1	Man Bahadur Bishwakarma	Nepali Congress	M	10591	Second Position
11.	Bara	3	Shree Prasad Paswan	Communist Party of Nepal (U.M.L.)	M	5708	Second Position
12.	Syangja	3	Khim Kumar B.K	Communist Party of Nepal (Maoist)	M	11136	Third Position
13.	Kapilvastu	5	Uma B.K	Communist Party of Nepal (Maoist)	F	7327	Third Position

All the political parties contesting election under the First Past the Post System submitted list of their candidates for the Proportional Representation System.

None of the contesting political parties had submitted a list of total seats. The Communist Party of Nepal (Maoist) and Rashtriya Janmorcha submitted a list of 333 candidates each. The Nepali Congress submitted a list of 329 candidates, CPN (UML) 332 candidates, Communist Party of Nepal (United) 328 and Janmorcha Nepal 320 candidates. The Madheshi Janadhikar Forum submitted a list of 100 candidates and Tarai Madheshi Loktantrik Party 97 candidates only. 17 political parties were such which had submitted list of less than 50 candidates.

The Communist Party of Nepal (Maoist) received the highest number of votes i.e. 3144204. The Nepali Congress received 2269883 votes and UML 2183370 votes.

Table No – 19

Votes Secured by Four Main Political Parties Under Proportional Representation

S.No.	*Party*	*Votes Secured*
1.	CPN (Maoist)	3149204
2.	UML	2183370
3.	Nepali Congress	2269883
4.	Madheshi Janadhikar Forum	678327

Table No – 20

Final Position in the Constituent Assembly

S.No.	*Party*	*FPTP*	*PR*	*Total*
1.	CPN (Maoist)	120	100	220
2.	Nepali Congress	37	73	110
3.	CPN (UML)	33	70	103
4.	MJM	30	22	55
5.	TMLP	9	11	20
6.	Sadbhawana Party	4	5	9
7.	NMKP	2	2	4
8.	Janmorcha Nepal	2	5	7
9.	Rashtriya Janmorcha	1	3	4

10.	Rashtriya Janshakti Party		3	3
11.	Rashtriya Prajatantrik Party		8	8
12.	CPN (ML)		8	6
13.	CPN (Joint)		5	4
14.	Rashtriya Prajata ntra Party Nepal		4	2
15.	Rashtriya Janmukti Party		2	2
16.	CPN (United)		2	2
17.	Nepal Sadbhawana Party (A)		2	2
18.	Nepali Jantadal		2	2
19.	Sanghiya Loktantrik Rashtriya Morch		2	1
20.	Samajbadi Prajatantra Janta Party, Nepal		1	1
21.	Dalit Janta Party		1	1
22.	Nepal Pariwar Dal		1	1
23.	Nepal Rashtriya Party		1	
24.	Nepal Loktantrik			
25.	Samajbadi Dal		1	1
26.	Chure Bhawar Rashtrya Ekta Party		1	1
Total		**240**	**335**	

Summing Up

Formation of the Constituent Assembly was a complex task which the interim government of Nepal could complete ultimately. Apart from the obvious political forces and factors working against the political change in Nepal and raising doubts about the sincerity of the government there were many structural and procedural issues.

The question of electoral system was raised. First the understanding was that the conventional system used by Nepal in the form of First Past The Post System would be applied. Later it was demanded that it should be replaced by Proportional Representation System. Ultimately it was decided that both the electoral systems will be applied. It was for the first time that elections were to be held in Nepal on the basis of both the systems.

Another issue that came up was regarding the strength of the Constituent Assembly. Initially it was to be a 425 member body. Later on, its strength was raised to 525 members. But taking into consideration the Tarai agitation and there demand for larger representation to Madheshis, strength of the Constituent Assembly was raised to 601.

The actual date of elections to the Constituent Assembly also became controversial. Initially, the elections were to be held in mid 2007. Later the elections were postponed to November 2007. But again the elections were deferred due to misunderstanding between the Maoists and the Seven Party Alliance. The postponement of elections for the second time was taken seriously not only by the Maoists and the Nepalese civil society but also by the international community. The announcement of fresh dates of elections after the December 23, 2007 agreement was a great relief to all. It was significant that Nepal for the first time experienced elections for a Constituent Assembly. These elections are important also for the reason that the Constituent Assembly will also function as Parliament till a new constitution is framed.

The Constituent Assembly election results exhibit some significant trends. The Maoists though could not seek majority emerged as the largest party. That way they are going to have a significant say in the government and the framing of the constitution.

The younger generation of the Nepalese politicians has find their way to law making body in a considerable way.

What is more significant is the inclusive character of the Constituent Assembly. There is significant representation from the ethnic groups, women, dalits and the Madheshi above all. If these are any indications the question of inclusive democracy, federalism, regional autonomy are nearing resolution in Nepal.

References

1. *Nepali Congress Manifesto*, Central Publicity Committee, Kathmandu, 10 March, 2008: 16.
2. *n.1*: 12.
3. http//www.election.govnp/in/provelection.html
4. *Manifesto of the communist Party of Nepal* (Maoist), Kathmandu, 2008
5. *Manifesto the Communist party of Nepal*–UML.

5

Monarchy To Republican State: Abrogation of The Hereditary Kingship

The issue of restructuring of the state, looming largely in the minds of the Nepalese political actors for quite some time, reached to a final stage with the decision of the Constituent Assembly to declare Nepal a republican state. With this the monarchy's rule as a real power holder or as a constitutional head has come to an end. It is a significant beginning towards the realization of the goals of restructuring of state and society. The 239 years old institution of monarchy has been abolished. The institution of monarchy not only symbolized a powerful political institution but also an institution of high religio – cultural significance. The Monarchy also symbolized continuation of the traditional and feudal forces. The abolition of monarchy not only have political ramifications but it is bound to have wide ranging social and economic ramifications. What is more important is that it is a major landmark towards building a new democracy in Nepal.

Foundation of Hereditary Monarchy

The modern state of Nepal came into existence in 1769. Before that Nepal was divided into several small principalities. There were 46 small states in the east and the west of Kathmandu valley known as *Baise* and *Chaubisi* states, representing different ethno – religious groups and communities. These apart, there were tribal states of Kosi and Gandaki basins; Newar rulers of Kathmandu valley and the Sen of Palpa. Prithvinarain Shah a ruler of the Gurkha principality took up a military adventure and invaded and defeated various principalities and the rulers of Kathmandu.[1] He then founded the

Kingdom of Nepal in 1769. King Prithvinarain Shah was conscious of the fact that the new Kingdom had emerged through a process of a forced unification of diverse ethno – cultural groups that were hostile to and fighting with each other for their existence. It was indeed a matter of great consideration that these principalities had been brought together through a military expedition. It was not possible to sustain a kingdom on the basis of military power alone on a long-term basis. There was a need to evolve a socio – cultural milieu that would give shape to a monolithic social order in Nepal. There was also a need to evolve a strong socio – religious base for the rule of the king.

Before the advent of the Shah rule tribal societies divided into different clans and ribs existed in Nepal. These tribal societies were not monolith and they had diverse forms and systems.[2] King Prithvinarain Shah tried to define the state in religious – cultural terms[3] It was declared by the king that all the land resources of Nepal automatically rest under his possession and control. The land was identified as Desa (the country) and the people as *Realm*. The King was projected as the sovereign lord, and he had proprietary authority over both. The kingship was accorded a religious basis and was declared as the representative of Lord Vishnu and that way; he got the right to rule the Desa and the Realm both. Thus, the king was projected as sovereign over the land; the protector of his subjects and the territory and the source of all aspirations, rules and traditions.

King Prithvinarain Shah adopted a multi – dimensional approach in order to build a strong and unified Nepali society and state. He followed a stratified hierarchical model for the society based on the *Chaturvarna* Hindu caste system. The Brahmins and the Kshatriya were accorded top place in this hierarchical order. They were called *Tagadharis* who had the authority to wear the sacred thread and perform all kinds of religious rituals. Next in the hierarchy were the *Matwalis*. The *Matwalis* were devided into two categories: non-salvageable *Matwalis* and salvageable *Matwalis*. All the ethnic groups were classified under these categories. On the whole there were four *varnas* and *chattis jats* (Thirty six castes) Jung Bahadur Rana further classified them in his Mulki Ain of 1854. King Prithvinarain and his successors though accepted this cultural diversity never recognized cultural rights of these communities. They were not given any opportunity to articulate their rights and demands.[4]

The social set-up thus evolved had Brahminic supremacy. As a result, the Brahmins acquired social prestige and also gained supremacy in politico-economic and administrative fields. The Kshatriyas (Thakuris) had next place in the social hierarchy. They got positions in the royal palace. They were the protector of royal authority. As a result they enjoyed power, privileges by the king and hold over land. Thus, the fundamental conception about social groups were centripetal and hierarchical.[5]

What is important here is that in the hierarchical social order of Nepal, it were the Brahminis and Thakuris of the hill region who were accorded positions of power and privilege. This bowed seeds of regional disparities as well. Because it were the Brahmins and Thakuris of the hill region who became repository of the hill culture. Henceforth, identification with the hill culture and caste hierarchy became important in determining power and prestige of various social groups.[6] The people of Tarai were encouraged to follow the hill cultural traits[7], which they resented and consequently they got dissatisfied and felt being discriminated. Thus, there was no identification of the people of Tarai with the state. The differentiations between the hill and the Tarai people provided a negative definition for Nepali national identity.

The Shah rulers used the symbols and traits of Hinduism as a source of legitimization of their authority.[8] In order to provide it a broader social base they started a process of Hinduaization. They also believed that by taking various groups and communities within the fold of Hinduism Nepali will be developed as a monolithic society. The non-Hindu tribal communities were motivated as well as forced to accept the Hindu religion. They were categorized under the Hindu hierarchical four fier caste order. All tribal people were placed in the lowest web of this order. A policy of compensation and accommodation was also followed in order to bring non-Hindu communities within the fold of Hinduism. The Magars were allowed to wear scared thread as recognition to the services that they had rendered to the palace. King Prithvinarain Shah said, "I am the king of Magrant". It was indeed an emotional attempt to assimilate Magars. The Gurungs were also rewarded for the services rendered by them to the Gurkha rulers. Autonomy was also given to Limbus for sometime.

Monarchy accorded protection to Hindu temples and shrines. Crime was graded on the basis of caste and punishment was fixed accordingly. The Brahmins were excluded from capital punishment. Thus, Brahminic supremacy became hallmark of the Nepali state and society.

A unified religious and cultural policy was persuaded. Nepal was given the status of a Hindu state. King Prithvinarain Shah said 'Yo Asli Hindustan Ho' (This is the real Hindustan) The *Gorkhali* or the *Khas Kura* was designated as the language of Nepal in the form of Nepali.

It is clear that the Nepali rulers followed a policy of forced cultural unification of different ethnic groups. Efforts were made to bring various tribal groups, belonging to the Mongoloid racial stock under the fold of Hinduism. It served dual objectives of social and political order.[9] The institution of monarchy was a rallying point between the high caste Hindus of the hills and the ethnic groups. It may also be pointed out here that the Nepali rulers deliberately kept various communities isolated and underdeveloped. Actually, the ruling elite wanted to lay-down a foundation of a unified model under the framework of Hinduism. Obviously, no efforts could be made towards the socio-economic uplifting of backward communities, assuming that it would generate consciousness among them, ultimately being detrimental to the authoritarian rule of the monarchy and the Ranas. The state thus emerged in Nepal has been viewed by scholar as a predatory Hindu state.

Decline of Shah Kings

The Shah rulers laid a strong foundation of monarchy in Nepal through internal consolidation and external expansion. But they could not prevent a gradual erosion of the central authority of the king. The powers slipped into the hands of the regent due to the ineffectiveness of the king or he being a minor or powers went in the hands of the Prime Minister. The palace became a focal point of conspiracies, and intrigues. A tug of war had begun between various noble families to hold power. After 1801 Damodar Pande and Bhism Sen Thapa emerged as the powerful Prime Ministers. The erosion of royal power was a gradual process, largely due to passing of power in the hands of the regents.

The shifting of powers from the king to the nobles caused emergence of various centres of power and authority that were rival to each other. It paved way for the emergence of Jung Bahadur Rana a junior official in the palace who took over powers through a conspiracy in 1846.

Jung Bahadur declared himself as the Prime Minister of Nepal and took all powers of monarchy in his hands. The king was made a virtual prisoner in the royal palace.[11] Thus, Jung Bahadur established family oligarchy of the Ranas. All the positions of power were filled from among the members of the Rana family. A system of hereditary Prime Ministership was established in Nepal.

The Rana rulers established a highly cartelized and authoritarian political system. It was basically a familial system in which all top positions were distributed among the family members of Ranas in a hierarchical order. Since the Ranas had come to power through a ghastly massacre, they established a reign of tyranny in the country. No rooms were left for any kind of opposition within the country. However, they could not prevent growth of opposition to their rule outside the country in India. The Rana system was dealt a fatal blow by the armed insurrection started by the Nepali Congress party during late 1950 and early 1951 with covert blessings of king Tribhuwan.

Restoration of Monarchy

After the abolition of the autocratic rule of the Ranas, the status and powers of the monarchy were restored. The traditional concept of legitimacy underwent modifications and the constitutional rule replaced the norms of power, authority and legitimacy. The monarchy expressed its commitment to establishment of democracy in Nepal. However, the constitutional concepts and democratic sentiments could not be realized during the period between 1951–1960. Some attempts were made by the modernizing political elite to introduce some of the political and legal forms of democracy. But these attempts failed in creating a broader space for democracy, largely due to feudalistic order of the society and the weak and fragmented political parties. It provided an edge to the assertion of powers by the monarchy, particularly after 1955 when king Mahendra a highly ambitions monarch took over the reigns of power.

First general elections were although held in 1959 but the experiment in parliamentary democracy proved to be short lived. The royal takeover of 15 December 1960 was marked by the restoration of monarchic rule in the country. The king once again became source of all political powers. The concept of popular democracy based on the notion of popular legitimacy and universal adult sufferage was subverted. King Mahendra wanted to retain all powers in his hands and act as an absolute monarch.

King Mahendra introduced panchayat system in 1962 which was basically aimed at providing a democratic cover to the royal political supremacy. The panchayat system ensured absolute autocratic authority of the king by making it a system devoid of political parties and organized political activities. King Mahendra tried to create a cultural myth about panchayats by propagating that the roots of this system were in the soil of the country and that it suited to the social and psychological climate of the country. But it is also a fact that king Mahendra also took utmost care in advocating that he had faith in the concept of popular sovereignty and that the panchayat system was based on the principles of democracy and decentralization. However, it was clear that the panchayat system had extremely limited scope for any meaningful direct participation of the people.

King Birendra who came to power in 1972 also believed in projecting the institution of monarchy as an absolute ruler. He followed the panchayat system installed in the country by his august father.

Establishment of Constitutional Monarchy

After the 1990 democratic movement an era of constitutional monarchy began in Nepal. 1991 the constitution envisaged constitutional monarchy in Nepal. The king became the head of the state. He was assigned emergency powers in the constitution. The first decade after the establishment of parliamentary democracy was crucial for Nepal as there was a fundamental change in the status and powers of the monarchy. Nevertheless, king Birendra tried to laiddown a foundation of monarchy as a constitutional head. The feudalistic order of the Nepalese society had not undergone much change. Therefore, the monarchy was still the most powerful institution. The political parties and leaders continuously looked towards the king for political support and privileges and for the resolution of political tangles. Still one would like to state that on the whole king Birendra tried to refrain himself from political interferences and thereby he tried to lay a foundation for constitutional monarchy. But the ghastly murder of king Birendra and his family on 1 June 2001 also abandoned this process.

King Gyanendra's Political Assertion

King Gyanendra after owning the throne in June 2001 began to search for an active role in politics.[12] He was highly ambitious and wanted to take powers in his hands. The king enjoyed support from the old nobility, bureaucracy, feudalistic sections of the society and the Royal Army. The political parties had proved to be weak and fragmented. The successive governments after 1996 had failed in finding a solution to the Maoist problem. The talks between the government and the Maoists held between August – November 2001 had failed and emergency had been imposed in the country on 26 November 2001. The Royal Nepal Army had been deployed to contain the Maoists. king Gyanendra held the government and the political parties responsible for the failure in tackling the Maoist problem. In fact, the political situation in Nepal went in favour of king Gyanendra because he was looking for such an opportunity to blame the government for its failures.

It may be pointed out here that immediately after ascending the throne in June 2001, king Gyanendra had made it clear that he would not be a silent king like his brother, who agreed to become a constitutional monarch. It shows that the new monarch had his own political designs. In February 2004, he said in a speech that the days when monarchy was not heard had gone. He gave the impression that the monarchy would no more remain a silent spectator. However, Gyanendra faced internal and international pressure for political liberalization. So he was compelled for yet another governmental change and once again appointed Sher Bahadur Deuba as Prime Minister of Nepal on 4 July, 2004. By appointing Deuba he tried to project that he was concerned for the restoration of democracy in the country. But such a step was taken just to pacify certain compelling factors. He continued holding powers and made all out efforts to control the political leaders, media and the civil society. Even the intellectuals who had been supporting democracy in their writings were not allowed to leave the place of their residence. It only indicates that king Gyanendra was trying to exert his full control over the country.

The Royal Takeover

King Gyanendra dismissed Sher Bahadur Deuba government on 1 February 2005 and declared a state of emergency in the country and assumed all powers of the government as an absolute monarch. It was a well thought of and planned decision taken by king Gyanendra. 'In his announcement king Gyanendra said that he will himself assume all powers and rule the country directly as Chairman of the council of ministers for a period of three years.[13] Gyanendra in fact, took advantage of the constitutional provision under article 19 of the 1990 constitution, which provided for emergency powers to the king. However, Gyanendra's action was uncalled for as there was no such urgency for declaring emergency in the country, except that he was looking for some opportunity to take over all powers in his hands directly. The kind of situation prevailed in the country had continued for last many years and, therefore, it was beyond the spirit of the constitution to use such provision without any reason.[14] It was not clear as what was the justification behind announcing king's direct rule for three years? It was certain that the king was highly ambitious. He wanted to become a real player of politics. But no one would have thought of such a drastic and early action by king Gyanendra. The Royal Nepali Army had full support to him and assisted the king in implementing his political motives.[15] He took a number of measures with a view to consolidate his authority. The civil rights provided in the 1990 constitution were suspended.

King Gyanendra's assumption of powers followed a series of actions against his political adversaries. The main political leaders were house arrested or detained or placed in jails. All kind of communications such as media, radio and television were brought under control. The media persons, intellectuals and other persons of civil society who were considered to be the supporters of democracy were also arrested or they were compelled not to move outside their city or district. It is clear that king Gyanendra defied the 1990 constitution as well as democracy and imposed his personal despotism in the country. He alleged that the political parties had failed in containing violence, controlling corruption in the country and improving economic situation. The political parties had not taken any serious steps to control the Maoist problem. So the king was not at all happy with the political parties.[16] It was the same situation as in 1960, when king Mahendra accused the political parties for having failed in serving the cause of democracy and stability and himself took over powers for the interest of the Nepalese people. Gyanendra also alleged that the government had failed in holding the general elections. It seems that the king was trying to justify his action by holding the political parties responsible for all the problems that the country was faced with.

King Gyanendra wanted to create a support base, which would strengthen his despotic rule and at the same time dawn the democratic forces. The royal army was already supporting him. What he now needed to create was a political support base.

For this purpose he decided to take support of the old guards of the panchayat era. On 2 February king announced formation of a 10 member council of ministers. On 14 February he appointed Tulsi Giri and Kirti Nidhi Bisht as Vice Chairmen of the council of ministers. Interestingly, king brought back those leaders of the panchayat era who had been out of active politics since long. But they had been strong supporters of the monarchy. Thus king tried to return to panchayat era.[17]

The council of ministers in its first meting announced a 21-point programme. A Corruption Control Royal Commission was also formed to look in to the cases of corruption. It was an important instrument to take all the political adversaries and opponents to task. In order to establish its control over the district administration the king appointed Zonal Commissioners in all the 14 administrative zones and development regions, as was the practice under the panchayat system. King tried to consolidate his powers with the help of royal army and the panchayat era political leadership. Towards, the middle of the year he announced withdrawal of the emergency. But control over media and communication, etc continued. Actually, it was done just in order to satisfy the international community, which was pressurizing king to return to multi-party democracy. King continued with its absolute control over the state powers.

King Gyanendra also tried to seek support from the international community in the name of controlling the Maoist insurgency. India, USA, UK and the other donor countries to Nepal though not happy with the action of king Gyanendra, continued to support him over the issue of armed action against the Maoists. Nepal also sought support from China, Pakistan, Russia, etc.

Maoists and Monarchy

The Maoists considered monarchy as a powerful repository of the feudalistic order of the Nepalese society. Even after the dawn of democracy they believed that the monarchy was all powerful and they strongly opined that it would not be possible for democracy to take roots in the country so long the monarchy would continue to play a role in the politics of Nepal. Therefore, the Maoists believed that the ultimate goal was a republican state. The Unity Centre did no favour constitutional monarchy in 1990. However, in 1996 when the Communist Party of Nepal (Maoists) submitted its 40 point demand charter they did not make any direct reference to the abolition of monarchy. Instead they talked of a republican state, which indirectly meant abolition of the monarchy. It was said in the demand charter that all the special rights and privileges of the king and his family should be withdrawn.[18]

Once the Maoist movement began gap between the monarchy and the Maoists widened day by day. They became more and more vocal about the institution of monarchy. The Maoists began to agree that the institution of monarchy was not something rooted in the Nepalese society and culture. Rather it had been imposed on the people by the rulers and all traits related to the institution of monarchy were designed in order to establish its absolute rule over the country.[19]

After the failure of the 2001 talks between the Maoists and the government, the former became forthright in their demand for the abolition of monarchy and declaring Nepal a republican state.

It was rightly said in an approach paper thus:

"The democratic movement of the Nepalese people against absolute monarchy, going on for more than half a century is now heading towards a climax. Whereas the eight year long people's War led by the CPN (Maoist) for a people's republic has virtually wiped out the feudal social – economic and cultural roots of the monarchy from the vast rural areas, the students affiliated to the major parliamentary parties, so far committed to the constitutional monarchy, have now switched over to the slogan of a republic and are spearheading the movement in the urban areas. This historical confluence of the two currents of the democratic movement i.e. – revolutionary and parliamentary, for the abolition of the monarchy and internationalization of the republic has opened an excellent prospect for continuation of the anti monarchy democratic movement in the country."[20]

The Maoists condemned the royal takeover of February 2005. They viewed it as strengthening of the feudal forces. It seems that king Gyanendra was aware of the fact that the Maoists would not accept his takeover of powers and therefore would retaliate by increasing their attacks. So the Royal Army began to consolidate its actions against the Maoists. But at the sametime, Gyanendra was also concerned about his political motives. He wanted to give the impression that he was much concerned about the insurgency and was looking for a solution to this problem. He asked the Maoists to surrender their arms and return to the mainstream politics. It was made clear that those who would follow this direction would be rewarded and those who do not follow it would face a military action. King Gyanendra said in a statement that;

"We call upon all those who have gone astray, taking up arms against the nation and the people, and those who are engaged in criminal activities against peace and democracy to return to the mainstream of national politics peacefully. Ensuring opportunities to freely express one's views with patriotism as the focal point. Fulfilling one's aspirations and contributing with, welfare of the nation and people are the inter alia features of multiparty democracy. We assure all those who avail of this opportunity to join the national mainstream that the state will give them opportunities and rights equal to those enjoyed by our citizens without any discrimination whatsoever, neither the people nor the law will tolerate any terrorist activities against the state or its citizens."[21]

King Gyanendra though asked the Maoists to surrender and join the mainstream politics did not propose for any short of peaceful negotiations with them. He was not prepared for that indeed. It is also a fact that the Maoists were not in any illusion as far as the motives of king Gyanendra were concerned, therefore, they did not expect any soft attitude from him. The Maoists called for a 3 days strike in February 2005 and than 11 days long strike in April 2005. The Maoists and the king were aware of each other's intentions and goals and hence, there was no possibility of any thaw between the two.

Political Parties and Monarchy

King Gyanendra adopted a confrontationist attitude towards the political parties and was not prepared to negotiate with them as well. He was critical of the working of the political parties and blamed them for not taking the Maoist problem seriously. King Gyanendra, as stated earlier, also held them responsible for mis-governance, corruption and for weakening the process of national integration.

King's action against the leaders of various political parties further pulled them apart. The royal take over of February 2005 had already created a hiatus between the monarchy and the political parties. The disgusted political parties began to search possibilities for a united struggle against the king's takeover. In May 2005 seven political parties including the NC, UML, NC (D), Janmorcha Nepal,

NWPP, ULF and NSP (Anandi Devi) agreed to form an alliance to fight against the despotic rule of the king. The Seven Party Alliance (SPA) agreed on a 6 point programme that included restoration of the House of Representatives and the 1990 constitution, management of conflict, progressive movement for the restoration of democracy on the basis of 1990 constitution, adherence to multi-party democracy and elections for a Constituent Assembly.[22]

The SPA gave a call to do away with the autocratic rule of the monarchy. They had accorded top priority to the restoration of the House of Representatives. However, it was doubtful if this would help in resolving the political tangle in Nepal. It was pointed out by many that SPA had chalked out a weak agenda[23]. For the Maoists the more important issues were formation of the Constituent Assembly and declaring Nepal a republican state. It was not clear if the restoration of the 1999 parliament would ultimately lead to the process of formation of the Constituent Assembly. Nevertheless, the Seven Party Alliance was the first major attempt of the political parties against the royal take over. It also paved a way for the polarization of the democratic forces. It also gave a positive message to the civil society. On the whole it was a significant development and generated new hopes among the democratic forces of Nepal. It is thus clear that the royal coup of February 2005 pulled the political parties and the king apart. The political parties realized that it was not possible to sustain democracy in the longrum with monarchy playing a central political role. It is true that the political parties were still not clear about the future status of monarchy but a hiatus had been created between the two. The Maoists also wanted to pull the political parties and the monarchy apart. To this extent they succeeded.

International Response to King's Takeover

The international community though supporting the Nepali government against the Maoist insurgency did not like the royal coup of 2005. India, the United Kingdom and the United States of America expressed strong reactions over the king's takeover. The British government recalled its Ambassador to Nepal. On 9 February 2005 the Indian Ambassador to Nepal met King Gyanendra and urged him to return to multi party democracy. On 25 February 2005 India decided to suspend its military aid to Nepal till the country would return back to the democratic process. India's the than foreign minister Natwar Singh said in the parliament on 4th March 2005 that:

"The developments in Nepal constitute a serious set back to democracy and bring the monarchy and mainstream political parties in direct confrontation with each other. This can only benefit the forces that not only wish to undermine democracy in Nepal but the institution of democracy as well."[24]

The US Assistant Secretary in the Department of State, Donald Camp visited Nepal from 26-28 June 2008. He said that the king's action was not acceptable to the United States. The United States welcomed the formation of the Seven Party Alliance. The United Nations Organization was also not happy with the royal takeover of February 2005.

Depositioning the King

After the restoration of democracy in mid 2006 and the consequent SPA-Maoist understanding serious thoughts were being given to curtail powers of the king. In fact, the people of Nepal had faced lot of atrocities during the period of direct rule of the king. So they had lost their faith and sympathy towards king Gyanendra. They were not only interested in withdrawal of powers of the monarchy but his status and rule was also being questioned.

The interim government took a number of steps to curtail powers of the king. The position of monarchy as head of the state and chief of the army was abolished. Privileges given to the king were curtailed by the parliament. The concept of king in the parliament was also withdrawn. The necessity for the royal assent of the bills was withdrawn. The assets of king Gyanendra were brought under the perview of taxation. The 8 November 2006 agreement between the political parties and the Maoists effectively stated that the king had to be devoid of all political and administrative rights.

It can be said here that king Gyanendra's attempt to take power in his hands seriously harmed the institution of monarchy in Nepal. The dignity and influence of the monarchy was seriously eroded.[25] The king was gradually sidelined from the public life. Not only leftist and rightist political parties, but some of the royalist political parties also began to criticize the role of the king. The political parties like Rashtriya Prajatantra Party known to be a pro-panchayat party, became critical of Gyanendra's role. There were differences among political parties regarding the line of action to be taken and the future of monarchy. But it is certain that the monarchy had become a main target of criticism among the political parties as well as the civil society.

In the context of the atrocities done by King Gyanendra there was an atmosphere building up against him and all agreed and supported the idea of curtailing powers of the king. However, on the question of future of monarchy there were no clear perceptions except the one followed by the Maoists. Even the Nepali Congress party was not clear on this issue and its leaders gave contradictory statements at different points of time. The Maoists were of course clear that there was no future of monarchy in Nepal. However, initially they thought that it would not be easy to abolish the institution of monarchy. But gradually their view was strengthened with the actions being taken against the monarchy.

It is a different matter that king Gyanendra was not prepared to accept that he had committed atrocities on people. He still believed that he did no wrong and continued to rely upon the support of the old guards of panchayat period, army, feudal classes, etc. In his democracy day address, Gyanendra said that, "It is clear that the prevailing situation compelled us to take the 1 February 2005 step in accordance with the people's aspirations ......"[26] It was, however, certain that some of the established norms and practices were being ignored and that was sufficient to exhibit that the king was loosing ground very fast. The Prime Minister and the army chief did not accompany the king and the queen at the Indrajatra and Phulpati festivals. He was no more supposed to assent acts of parliament and receive credentials of the Ambassadors. His car was stoned when he visited Pashupatinath temple. These were some instances which took place for the first time and it only indicated that an atmosphere was building up against king Gyanendra.

Commission Against Gyanendra

The government constituted a commission under the chairmanship of justice Krishna Jung Raimajhji to recommend action against 202 persons including king Gyanendra who had been accused of committing atrocities on people after the 2005 royal takeover. Justice Raimajhi submitted its report to the government on 20 November 2006. The commission held king Gyanendra responsible for the atrocities on the people at the time of April 2006 pro-democracy movement. It was also recommended that action be taken against king Gyanendra not in his capacity as the king but as the then head of the state. The chairman of the committee said, "We have decided to recommend the parliament to take necessary steps against the king as we found him guilty.[27] It was also clarified that though king Gyanendra did not respond to the questions send by the commission it does not mean to say that he did not do any wrong. It is for the first time that a commission was constituted against the king of Nepal.

It is clear that the institution of monarchy had lost all its credibility and significance. As far king Gyanendra was concerned there were still people and groups in Nepal which looked for a minimum status to the monarchy in the new political set up, but it was difficult to reverse the trends. It can be said that the role played by king Gyanendra had proved to be detrimental to the institution of monarchy in Nepal. It seems that king Gyanendra in his capacity as the head of the state had to pay for all that happened during his direct rule. Not only that his powers were withdrawn but the facilities provided to him were either withdrawn or seriously curtailed. His personal property was brought under scrutiny. The Maoists were quite desperate to see an end to the monarchy as early as possible. It was also decided that the monarchy would be abolished if the king was found conspiring against elections to the CA.[28] The king and members of the royal family were also asked to declare their property and provide details about their personal accounts in banks in Nepal and abroad.[29] In the budget for the year 2007-2008 it was decided not to provide any allowance to the king and the members of the royal family. Earlier there was a provision of an allowance of Rs.18.7 million for the king and the royal family.

Provisions in the Interim Constitution

In part 23 of the interim constitution relating to transitional arrangements the following provisions were made regarding the king:

1. No powers regarding the governance of the country shall be vested in the king.
2. Instead, powers pertaining to the government shall be vested on the Prime Minister.
3. It was said that not withstanding anything contained elsewhere in this constitution, the Constituent Assembly in its first meeting shall take decision on the basis of a simple majority whether or not to give continuation to the monarchy.
4. The property of late king Birendra, late queen Aishwarya and other members of their family shall be brought under the control

of the government of Nepal, and a trust shall be established to use the property for the benefit of the nation.

5. All the property acquired by king Gyanendra in the capacity of the king of Nepal (palaces in different parts of the country, forests, national parks, heritage sites of historical and anthropological importance, etc.) shall be nationalized.

The interim constitution made a number of provisions to curtail the powers of the king.

The Maoists and the Seven Party Alliance had reached to the understanding that the Constituent Assembly would finally decide about the question of declaring Nepal a republican state. But the postponement of elections to the Constituent Assembly for twice in May 2007 and November 2007 disappointed the Maoists. They began to demand after mid 2007, that Nepal should be declared a republic an state and that monarchy be abolished before elections to the Constitutional Assembly would be held. They withdrew from interim government over this issue. A serious deadlock was again created to the peace process. But in the December 2007 agreement it was agreed that Nepal will become a republican state but a formal decision in this regard will be taken by the Constituent Assembly in its first meeting. On 28 December 2007 the legislature – parliament of Nepal formally approved a motion to abolish the monarchy and declare Nepal a federal Democratic Republic. The motion was approved by a majority of 270 members out of 329. This decision ended the deadlock between the Maoists and the government and the Maoists once again joined the interim government.[30]

Declaration of the Republican State

The Constituent Assembly in its first meeting held on 28 May 2008 took its historical decision to abolish the 239 years old institution of monarchy in Nepal and declare it a federal, democratic republic.

Home Minister, Krashna Prasad Sitaula tabled the proposal to abolish the monarchy and in the house of 560 members 572 supported the proposal. Only 4 members voted in favour of the continuation of monarchy. It clearly indicates that almost every party in the Constituent Assembly was in favour of the republican state. King Gyanendra was given 15 days time to leave the Narayan Hity Royal Palace.

The developments that took place after the 2005 royal takeover lead to fast decline of monarchy. In a way the roots of the decline of monarchy had been laid in the murder of king Birendra in 2001. There were many who believed that the hereditary monarchy had ended with the death of King Birendra. There were a large number of people in Nepal who lost their religio-cultural faith on monarchy after this incident. But the political ambitions of king Gyanendra proved to be fatalistic. The royal coup not only convinced the Maoists that their objectives would not be realized so long as this feudal order would continue but it also turned the political parties against the king.

It is believed by some that the destiny was like that. The abrogation of the Shah dynasty had been scripted centuries ago. It is said that Guru Gorakhnath had told king Prithvinarayan Shah that the Shah rulers will rule the country till 11 generations. Incidentally Gyanendra happened to be the 11th descendant of Prithvi Narayan Shah. It might be true or a coincidence but the fact remains that the monarchy has ended in Nepal. It is also true to say that whatever other reasons might have been, king Gyanendra's own acts and omissions were largely responsible for the abrogation of monarchy in Nepal.

It may also be pointed out here that the abrogation of monarchy is an important milestone in the political history of Nepal. It not only symbolized abolition of monarchy but also abolition of the feudalistic order of the Nepalese society and polity. Feudalism had survived in Nepal in one way or the other due to the institution of monarchy. Now it opened way not only for political but social transformation as well.

References

1. For details see, Ram Niwas Pandey, *Making of Modern Nepal,* Nirala, New Delhi, 1997; D.R. Regmi, *Modern Nepal,* Firma K.L. Mukhopadhyay, Calcutta, 1961; B.C. Sharma, *Nepal Ko Etihasik Ruprekha,* Krishnakesmari Devi, Varanasi, V.S. 2022.
2. R.S.Chauhan, *Society and State Building in Nepal,* Sterling Publishers, New Delhi, 1989: 1-23.
3. Richard Burghart, *The conditions of Listening, Essays on Religion, History and Politics in South Asia,* Oxford University Press, Delhi, 1996:194-226.

4. Prayag Raj Sharma, *The State and Society in Nepal, Historical Foundations and Contemporary Concerns,* Himal Books, Lalitpur, 2004: 212.
5. David N. Gellner, "Ethnicity and Nationalism in the World's Only Hindu State", in David N.Gellner et. Al. (eds.), *Nationalism and Ethnicity in a Himalayan Kingdom, The Politics of Culture in Contemporary Nepal,* Harvard Academic Publishers, Amsterdam, 1997: 4-5.
6. Ramakant & B.C.Upreti, "Regionalism in Nepal" in Ramakant (ed.), *Regionalism in South Asia,* Aalekh Publishers, Jaipur, 1983 : 138-160.
7. See, Fredrik H. Garge, *Regionalism and National Unity in Nepal,* California University Press, Berkeley, 1975.
8. John Whelpton, "Political Identity in Nepal: State, Nation and Community," in David N. Gellner **n.5**: 43-44.
9. Harka Bahadur Gurung, *Nepal, Social Demography and Expression,* New ERA, Kathmandu, 1998: 88.
10. Harka Bahadur Gurung, "State and Society in Nepal", in David N.Gellner (ed.) **n.5**: 465-472.
11. See, Kusum Shreshtha, *Monarchy in Nepal, Tribhuwan Era,* Popular Prakashan, Bombay, 1984, Also See, Rishikesh Shaha, *Three Decades and Two Kings,* Sterling Publishers, New Delhi, 1990.
12. See, B.C.Upreti, *Nepal, Democracy at Cross Road,* Kanishka Publishers, Distributors, Delhi, 2007.
13. For the text of his speech see, *The Kathmandu Post,* February 2, 2005.
14. Manjushree Thapa, "Nepal's Troubled Kingdom", *The Hindu,* April 23, 2006.
15. Michael Hutt, "Nepal and Bhutan in 2005, Monarch and Democracy Can They Coexist"?, *Asian Survey,* Vol. XLVI, No.1, January – February, 2006: 120.
16. See, *The Kathmandu Post,* February 2, 2005.
17. Michael Hutt, **n.15**: 121.
18. International Crisis Group, *Nepal's Maoists: Their Aims, Structure and Strategy,* Asia Report No. 104, 27 October, 2005: 4-5.
19. See, *Some Important Documents of Communist Party of Nepal (M),* Janadesh Publication, Kathmandu, 2004.
20. Approach Paper on "Relevance of Monarchy in Nepal", presented at the Nepalese People's Right Protection Committee, New Delhi, 12 February, 2004.

21. Bishnu Raj Upreti, *Armed Conflict and Peace Process in Nepal,* Adroit Publishers, Delhi, 2006: 325.
22. *The Kathmandu Post,* May 9, 2005.
23. Bishnu Raj Upreti, *n.21*: 348.
24. *n.21.*
25. See, International Crisis Group, *Peace Agreement: Making It Work,* Asia Repot No. 126, 15 December, 2006: 20.
26. King Gyanendra's Democracy Day Address, *The Kathmandu Post* 11 February, 2007.
27. *The Hindu,* June 15, 2006
28. *The Hindustan Times,* April 3, 2007.
29. *The Statesman,* March 13, 2007.
30. *The Statesman,* December 31, 2007.

6

Changing Paradigm of Nepali Politics: Issues, Challenges and Prospects

Nepal is among those countries of South Asia which have been shifting from one kind of political system to another. It was way back in 1950 that Nepal stepped on the path to political modernization and development. For the first time, Nepal moved on the path to democracy in 1950. This experiment in parliamentary democracy under the leadership of monarchy continued for the whole decade of the fifties. In 1959 Nepal succeeded in installing a western styled parliamentary democracy. But it could not be sustained for long and proved to be short-lived. In December 1960 king Mahendra took all powers in his hands by abrogating the infant democratic system. King's direct rule was established in the country subsequently.

In 1962 a new system called panchayat system was established under the overall leadership of the king. It continued nearly for 28 years and was overthrown in the 1990 democratic movement. The 1990 movement for democracy was indeed a major landmark in the contemporary political history of Nepal, as it laid foundation of constitutional monarchy in the country. The working of the democracy in the post 1990 period was marked by political instability, misgovernance and weakening of the democratic institutions. A major challenge to the state came in the form of the Maoist insurgency. It not only added to political instability and disorder but also created a reign of violence and fear in the country. This state of political instability and conflict took a new turn in October 2002, when king Gyanendra dismissed the elected government, suspended the parliament and began to search a role for himself in the politics of Nepal.

King Gyanendra's search for a political space reached to its final destination in February 2005, when through a royal coup he himself assumed all political powers. But the polarization of the political parties and the Maoists proved to be fruitful and democracy was restored in April 2006. It clearly shows that the Nepali politics has been continuously dominated by interplay of authoritarian and democratic forces. The democratic forces have been paralyzed at different points of time due to the political assertion of the authoritarian forces. The Maoist insurgency was in a way the result of the failure of democratic forces in sidelining the authoritarian and the feudal forces. Nevertheless, one would agree with the view that despite political assertion by authoritarian forces and their attempts to level democratic elite incompetent and advocating non suitability of western democracy for Nepal, democratic forces have survived. The democratic fervour of the Nepalese people have remained alive despite all shorts of onslaughts.

Between 2006 – 2007 developments took place quite fast towards the consolidation of peace process in the country. There were enough indications to explain that perhaps the Nepalese political leaders and parties have learned from the past experiences. A number of occasions came when the peace process would have been derailed. But the Seven Party Alliance showed enough resiliance and tried to adjust itself with the emerging situation. The Maoist approach to promote its political objectives by joining the multiparty democracy also proved to be fruit bearing and it opened opportunities for the revival of multiparty democracy.

Nepal is passing through a critical phase of political transition at the movement. The formation of the Constituent Assembly and declaring Nepal a republican state are two significant milestones in this transition. But it is only a beginning and a large number of issues are still to be resolved. Many of these issues are challenging and need a careful handling.

The formation of the government after the elections of the Constituent Assembly became a contentious issue as none of the political parties gained majority in the assembly. The Maoists emerged as the largest party but they did not have sufficient strength so as to form the government on its own. There three possibilities: Girja Prasad Koirala, Prime Minister of the interim government would continue with the support of other parties; the Nepali Congress and the CPN (Maoist) would form the government and that a multiparty coalition government would be formed. None of the major parties, however, took a clear stand on the issue of government formation and a situation of uncertainty continued for some time. Two major political parties: The Nepali Congress and the CPN (Maoist) failed in reaching to any consensus over this issue. There was utter confusion and the one party blamed the other for indecisiveness. It seems that the different political parties were not in a position to take any initiative as they did not have a clear mandate. But they also did not try to promote other political parties by supporting them. Thus the political parties lacked a clear perception and proper initiatives. G.P. Koirala on the other hand, refused to resign as Prime Minister of the interim government.

The Maoists also failed in forming a government on time. There was lot of confusion among the party leaders. At one stage the party supremo Prachanda said that in the election manifesto of the party he (Prachanda) had been projected as the first president of Nepal. At one stage the CPN (M) asserted for both the positions of the President and the Prime Minister. Actually, initially the CPN (M) appeared to be under the impression that since it was the largest party in the Constituent Assembly both the positions of the President and the Prime Minister should go to it. Therefore, while Prachanda was being projected as a candidate for the President Babu Ram Bhattarai was projected as party's candidate for the Prime Ministership. However, the largest parties the CPN (M), NC and UML failed in reaching to any consensus. Girja Prasad Koirala being the Prime Minister of the interim government had an important role to play in this regard. The Maoists were of the opinion that Koirala needed to play the role what Sonia Gandhi has been playing in India. It was stated that:

"We do not want Koirala to step down or resign. Rather we want him to be the guardian of the new coalition and guide it at every step. Actually we want him to play a political role similar to Sonia Gandhi in the United Progressive Alliance government in India"[1]

It is difficult to say whether G.P. Koirala was prepared to take up any such kind of role. The UML was also silent over the issue of formation of the government. In the mean times elections for the office of the President and Vice-President were held. The Nepali Congress candidate won as President in the second round of polling in the CA and Madhesh Janadhikar Forum candidate for Vice President. These were also not free of party politics.

The issue of the formation of the government was ultimately decided by the Constituent Assembly. The CPN (M) put Prachanda as its candidate for Prime Minister while the Nepali Congress nominated Sher Bahadur Dueba, senior leader and three time Prime Minister of Nepal as its candidate. Shere Bahadur Dueba got only 113 votes while Prachanda secured 464 votes. Thus Prachanda was elected as Prime Minister.

The other 21 political parties elected to the Constituent Assembly announced their support to the CPN (M), while the People's Front of Nepal and Nepal Worker's and Peasants Party boycotted the election. The CPN-UML and the Madhesi Janadhikar Forum joined the cabinet. The Nepali Congress, the second largest party in the Constituent Assembly decided to remain in the opposition. However, the party leaders have accused each other for delays, distrust and indecisiveness. The formation of the government was an important issue and it did not lead to any kind of breakdown. The CPN (M) chief wanted to seek assurance of the Constituent Assembly that the government will not be pulled down for two years. It was indeed important in the context of consolidation of peace process. Because the whole issue of the exercise in constitution making would rest on the governmental stability and cooperation of the political parties. It may be noted here that the way the process of formation of the government went on it clearly reflected upon the desire of the political parties to Share power, and at the same time to ensure their identity in the emerging political set up.

II

The Constituent Assembly is an important factor in taking the peace process further in Nepal and realize the ultimate goal of building a new democracy in Nepal. The Constituent Assembly has to perform dual functions. It has to perform the role of the national legislature and also to frame a new constitution for the country. As has been said earlier, none of the political parties have secured majority in the Constituent Assembly. The CPN (M), NC and UML are the major actors along with the Tarai based political parties. It has its positive and negative implications. Much would depend on the consensus that these political parties would be able to build with regard to several significant issues. The cooperative efforts are some time fruit bearing, if all the parties agree to such efforts. In the present context a single party is not in a position to dictate the functioning of the Constituent Assembly. It is a positive development in many respects. But it is equally important to what extent the largest party the CPN (M) is in a position to seek cooperation from the other political parties.

It is important to note that the set up of the Constituent Assembly is much different from the earlier character of the legislature. It can be said that for the first time as elected representative, the representative political institution has obtained an inclusive character in Nepal. It is true that this inclusive character is not absolute but there is a fundamental change from the previous parliaments. Significantly, 25 political parties have secured representation in the Constituent Assembly. There is also significant regional, ethnic, gender, caste and dalit representation in the Constituent Assembly. It is indeed a significant development and adds to the representative character of the elected bodies. However, it can be observed that most of the Dalit elected representatives and majority of the women representatives in the Constituent Assembly belong to the CPN (M). Nevertheless, it is an important headway even if only one political party has been able to actualize it.

The entry of Madheshi parties in the Constituent Assembly is also a major development. It is for the first time that the Tarai region of Nepal has got representation in a national political institution in such an impressive number. One would hope that it is a small beginning towards reducing gap between hills and Madhesh on several counts. The joining of Madheshis in the national politics would also change the nature and direction of the Nepalese politics. The Madheshis had been deprived of their proper representation in politico–administrative structures and armed forces. The term Madheshi itself has been a some what unpleasant term used by the hill people for the people of Tarai. One may say that with the wider opportunities opening for the people of Tarai such kind of feelings may also be diminished.

It is also important to note that the political parties that have been viewed as royalist and had been supporting the monarchy are wiped out in the Constituent Assembly. Political parties like Rashtriya Prajatantra Party and its splinter groups could not secure any seat of the Constituent Assembly under the Fast Past the Post System. It got representation under the Proportional Representation System only on the basis of votes secured by it. It is not anything significant taking into account the past political background of these parties. Many Prime Ministers and important leaders of the panchayat and post panchayat era have been associated with these parties. It is indeed a sufficient indication towards the rejection of the royalist parties by the people. It does not matter what they have secured under the proportional representation. Even political parties like Nepal Pariwar Dal or Chure Bhavar Ekta Samaj got a seat in the Constituent Assembly on the basis of votes secured by them under the Proportional Representation System.

A number of old guards have been rejected by the voters in the Constituent Assembly elections. Madhav Kumar Nepal, Bamdev Gautam, Chakra Bastola, Rajendra B. Amatya and many others were defeated.

The Constituent Assembly is a change in many respects in the electoral history of Nepal. It has in fact for the First time acquired an inclusive character – an important break through indeed towards rebuilding democracy in Nepal.

III

What took the Maoists to the victory stand through the process of multi party democracy is a significant issue here. In a very little time of two years, the Maoists have moved from an underground insurgent group to the largest political party in the Constituent Assembly. The Maoists have gone ahead of the Nepali Congress a party of long standing in Nepalese politics and the United Marxist Leninist party. What attributed to the success of the Maoists?

In 2006 the Maoists took a 'U' turn and decided to join the mainstream politics. They began to support the constitutional – democratic path for the political transformation in Nepal. There were many who did not believe that such a fundamental change was taking place in the Maoist strategy. Once the Maoists joined the mainstream politics they made all out efforts to realize their political goals. Despite the fact that only two years before they were indulged in guerrilla war, they succeeded in creating a positive image of their own. There were certain reasons behind it.

1. The Maoists were very clear about their political goals since the beginning. They were committed to the abolition of monarchy and declaring Nepal a federal republic; a new constitution for Nepal prepared by the Constituent Assembly and a secular state and inclusive democracy. In peace talks with the government earlier, they did not compromise over any of these demands.

After joining the mainstream politics in 2006, they constantly pleaded for these goals and saw to it that the Seven Party Political Alliance agrees to work jointly for the realization of these objectives and that they become the common goals of the democratic forces. In contrast to the Maoists, even the political parties like Nepali Congress, UML, etc were not clear over these issues. Some of the leaders even gave contradictory statements over the future of monarchy, etc.

2. The Communist Party of Nepal (Maoist) was not infected with the kind of internal dissensions and groupism that the other political parties have been faced with. There has been enough internal democracy within the party in comparison to the other political parties. The party is also not faced with leadership conflicts. Some differences had occurred within the party during 2004 but they were resolved. The Maoist party also has a strong ideological commitment, which the other political parties have lacked.
3. The Maoists also had the benefit of having a strong organizational structure and dedicated cadres. It helped them in launching an organized election campaign. The mobilization capacity of the Maoists has been well recognized. Their electoral campaign was much organized and well targeted.
4. The Maoists did not ignore any section of the society and tried to take all the communities and regions with them. They particularly concentrated on the deprived sections of the society like lower caste people, tribal communities of Tarai, dalits, ethnic groups, etc. It may be pointed out here that earlier most of the political parties had ignored these groups. Similarly women and youth became a significant part of the Maoist support base. The Maoists not only gave tickets to the leaders of these segments but also sought their active support.
5. One another benefit to the Maoists has been that they worked in certain areas for years and years. A number of Maoist leaders carried underground activities in the mid western region of Nepal and created their strong bases. There are a number of districts in the mid western and far western region where no other party could capture a single seat other than the Maoists. It clear by indicates that the Maoists had groomed these areas. Rukam, Rolpa, Dolpa, Salyan, etc are the areas where the Maoists made a clear sweep. It can be said that the Maoists had cultivated these constituencies which other parties could not.

IV

As pointed earlier Nepali politics has entered into a new phase after the formation of the Constituent Assembly elections. Till the formation of the Constituent Assembly elections the major issues were elections of CA, abolition of monarchy, republican state, and federalism. Now the main target is to actualize these and other related issues in a politico – constitutional framework. Therefore, the present phase is much more challenging and complex. There are a large number of issues and now the time has come when the Nepalese government and the Constituent Assembly has to face them and resolve them.

The Communist Party of Nepal (M) has formed the government under the leadership of Pushp Kamal Dahal 'Prachanda'. The sustenance of the government till a new constitution is framed would depend on a proper understating and cooperation between CPN (M), UML, MJF and the other partners of the coalition on the one hand and the Nepali Congress on the other. The earlier efforts towards a left unity had failed in Nepal. How long the CPN (M) – UML understanding will work can not be said definitely. The UML has been struggling, over the years, for its identity as the main proponent of the communist ideology in Nepal. It was not only challenged by the Maoists but thrown in the back yard. Will the UML be able to regain that status in collaboration with the Maoists is a moot question. The Tarai based parties have their own agenda. They are more concerned with the autonomy question and federalism. The Nepali Congress has opted to sit in the opposition. The Nepali Congress party has a long history of struggling for democracy in Nepal. It has been a party in power for several times. The Nepali Congress along with the other member parties of Seven Party Alliance came forward to collaborate with the Maoists in 2006. The party showed enough maturity and resilience in cooperating with the Maoists. There were ups and downs, delays and disturbances but the SPA – Maoists collaboration took the country upto the Constituent Assembly elections successfully. The Nepali Congress and the CPN (M) failed in reaching to any understanding in the post election phase towards forming a government. It was not uncalled for. But the point is to what extent the Nepali Congress is prepared to sit in opposition and play a constructive role? The fate of the coalition governments of the 1990's is an example how the political parties have behaved in the past. The question of identity is important for all the political parties.

What is the vision of the new constitution? A tone has been set by declaring Nepal a federal, democratic republic an state. It has already been accepted as a secular state. The actualization of these and other such issues within the politico – constitutional framework is a complex exercise. For instance, it is accepted that Nepal is going to be a federal state. The basis of creating federations is likely to be geography, ethnicity and language. The Maoists have already proposed to divide Nepal into 12 federations. Is federalism an answer to the crisis of nation building is one issue. It has also to be properly accessed that federalism is feasible for Nepal in terms of its geography, pluralism and uneven geographic situation and unequal resource distribution. The question of one Madhesh – One Pradesh is important. The Maoists talked of right to self determination. As a slogan it was alright. But the ground realities would be different. It has also to be noted that the experiences of other counties shows that ethnicity, regionalism and language are sensitive issues and the rise of ethno – regional and linguistic sentiments may become a continuous phenomenon.

The interim constitution of Nepal shows that on many issues the Maoists and the SPA took up a compromising attitude. But now instead of a compromise there is a need for a consensus among the political parties.

Have the Maoists aroused popular expectations in a big way? The Maoists gave high profile slogans in their manifesto such as to transform the Nepalese economy in a few years and raise it up to the level of the highly developed countries. The education, drinking, water, heath, etc are the much talked issues in the Maoist election agenda. Nepal has a poor economy. In a large part of the country people are still striving for the realization of basic needs. It has been a feudal economy to the core. The resource allocation and distribution system has so far benefited a small privileged class of the society. The Maoists had rightly talked of the need for the transformation of the Nepalese society and economy. Now they are at the helm of affairs. They have to work for the realization of popular expectations. There are three vital areas in this regard:

1. Fulfillment of basic needs: water, electricity, shelter, education and health.
2. Upbringing the depressed sections of the society.
3. Proper and adequate availability of goods of daily necessity.

There are also issues like land reforms, infra – structure development, corruption, etc which the Maoists have to deal with.

The CPN (M) lead coalition government has to work with a conservative bureaucracy that has so far been representing only a few privileged sections of the society. How it is going to be helpful in the implementation of the people oriented socio – economic agenda of the CPN (M) government is a big issue. There is an urgent need for restructuring the bureaucracy in terms of both its perceptional and foundational dimensions.

The Maoists combatants are still looking for their proper settlement. The issue has not yet been settled fully. Under the earlier provision they are living in cantonments in various parts of the country. But some solution has to be worked out regarding their future. Now can they be asked to go back to their homes? Will they not prove to be dangerous in that case? There are already dissatisfied persons and groups which have been talking up arms again. So this problem has to be properly dealt with. It can indeed become a source of further conflicts in Nepal. There has already been a proposal for their merger with the regular armed forces of Nepal. But a controversy has been raised in certain political circles in Nepal by arguing that the People's Liberation Army has been politically indoctrinated. On the other hand the senior officers of if it have warned of yet another conflict of if it is not merged with the Nepalese army. There is an urgent need to resolve this issue so as to consolidate the peace process.

There are three important parties in the Constituent Assembly with whom Maoists have to work as a party in the government. The Nepali Congress remains an important party in the Constituent Assembly and also the largest opposition party. Along with the Maoists credit goes to the Nepali Congress for the successful cooptation of the first phase of rebuilding democracy in Nepal. After the Constituent Assembly elections, however, the party seems to have reached to a critical phase of self – appraisal and need for restructuring itself. Was the Nepali Congress party prepared for such a performance in the elections? But the reality is like that and much of the conditions under which party has been functioning have been responsible for that. The party was once known for its strong commitment to democratic socialism. But over the years it left behind its ideological commitments and became oriented to power politics. The party has been far away from internal democracy. Groupism, leadership clashes; favouratism, etc have become the main features of the party. The notion of collective leadership proved to be a failure. The old guards of the party – Girija Prasad Koirala, Krishan Prasad Bhattarai have always indulged in factional politics even at the cost of the downfall of the party's government. Sher Bahadur Dueba left the NC party to form NC (D) but again joined the party sometimes before the elections. This itself speaks much about the factional politics in the party. The Nepali Congress was in power for many times after the beginning of the Maoist insurgency. It took a tough attitude towards the insurgents. But the political circumstances brought them together after a decade.

The support base of the party has declined and there has been an even sharper decline of its support base in the Tarai. The party needs to think over outlining a long term strategy for the future. It has to be understood here that for all the political parties of Nepal the present political transition is a test case for their performance in the elections to be held under the new constitution after two years or so.

The Communist Party of Nepal (UML) a moderate communist party emerged after the merger of some communist groups after the 1990 democratic revolution. The party has believed in multi – party democracy and was in power during 1994-1995. The rise of the Maoists has cornered the party in terms of representation of the communist ideology in the country. The party has lost its support base among factory workers, peasantry and the youth. It did not support the Maoists. The party seems to be more democratic. Madhav Nepal resigned after the elections and Jhal Nath Khanal joined as the new chief of the party.

The UML has joined the government. The party has to regain its support base. Can the CPN (M) and UML work together for a larger left unity is an important issue.

It is certain that there is a contest between the three but it is also a fact that the consolidation of the peace process is not possible without an understanding between the three parties. Prachanda as the Prime Minister of Nepal will have to work hard to maintain a proper balance between these parties along with Madhesh Janadhikar Forum. The Prachanda government has to take note of the fact that these parties form a major support base for him in the process of framing a new constitution for the country. The people of Nepal have seen political uncertainties and chiaos over the years. Those who have seen the governmental instability of the nineties and the fast chainging political scenario it is hard for them to believe that Nepali politics is on the way to sustainable peace, stability and democracy. The strikes, bundhs blockades had made the lives of the common people miserable. They blame political parties for all such conditions. There is a need for the government and the political parities to win their confidence. It is a big challenge for the Prachanda government indeed.

The external support structure is equally important. It is a fact that the Maoist insurgency aroused serious concerns among the international community. The Maoists were also declared as terrorists by the US government. The United States of America, the United Kingdom, India and other countries supported the Nepalese government in finding a military solution of the Maoist problem.

It is difficult for the countries like the United States to digest a Maoist government in Nepal. The Americans had congratulated the people of Nepal for the successful completion of the Constituent Assembly elections but they made no reference to the emergence of the CPN (M) as the largest party. The Maoists had viewed the United States as an expansionist power.

The Maoists also had inimical postures towards India during the course of insurgency. But there also existed several informal channels of interaction between the Maoist and the Indian political leaders. The situation took a turn after the 2005 royal coup. The Maoist leaders themselves played a role in softening party's attitude towards India. It also played a significant role in the Maoist – SPA understanding and the initiation of the peace process.

Now with the formation of the Prachanda government there are lots of specelations in India. Prachanda had stipulated that his party would like to develop friendly relations with both the neighbours. There is a general impression that the government of the Maoists will have a leaning towards China. Prachanda's first visits to China further added to these impressions. The Indian media projected it as Prachanda's natural tilt towards China. It is true that China is a close neighbour of Nepal. It is also true that the present government has its ideological parity with China. But relations with India are on a different platform. The history bears testimony to the fact that no other country can have an alternative to Nepal's relations with India.

Prime Minister Prachanda's first official visit is to New Delhi. was an important up towards clearing there misunderstandings. Any mature political leadership in Nepal would understand that the need of the hour is India's support in peace building not a conflicting relationship with that country. There are certain important issues between India and Napal, such as the revision of the 1950 Treaty of Peace and Friendship, mutual cooperation for water resources development, open border, migration, etc. These are such issues which can be taken up at a later stage. At the moment more important issues should be India's assistance for the socio – economic reconstruction in Nepal, Indian investments, joint ventures and trade. India's approach should be to build its confidence on the new government in Nepal. What inputs India can provide for Nepal's exercise on new constitution making, federalism, etc appear is be more important issues at the moment.

Lastly, what role the civil society can play in the development of sustainable peace and democracy in Nepal? In Nepal civil society has been weak and fragmented. However, certain civil society organizations have played an active role in the last few years. The civil society has to rise above political lineage and take up a constant stock of the efforts being made towards sustainable peace. The civil society organizations, the media and the intellectual community of Nepal has to play their role of checks and balances so that the process of constitution making takes place unabatedly. The future of Nepalese democracy rests on that.

Reference

1. *The Hindustan Times*, June 4, 2008.

APPENDIX - I

Population Structure of Nepal 2001

S.No.	Regions	Total Population	Male	Female	Percent
1	Mountain	1687859	837060	850799	7.29
2	Hill	10251111	5016802	5234309	44.28
3	Tarai	11212453	5710059	5502394	48.43
	Nepal	23151423	11563921	11587502	100.00

Source : Census of Nepal : 2001, HMG, Kathmandu

APPENDIX - II

Rules of Registration of Political Parties

Nepal's Constitution requires political parties to register with the Election Commission in order to stand for election. There are certain conditions that the Election Commission requires political parties to fulfill for registration.

The Interim Constitution of Nepal (2007) calls for the following provisions for a political party to register with the Election Commission:

1. Any political party wishing to secure recognition from the Election Commission for the purposes of election shall be required to register its name with the Election Commission as per the procedure determined by the Commission.
2. Parties applying for registration should have a written constitution and manifesto.
3. Parties shall clarify the other details such as: the name of the party, office of its central office, names and addresses of the members of its executive committee.
4. Parties must be democratic.
5. The party must be committed to the principles established in the Constitution of Nepal.
6. The party must uphold the sovereignty, unity and integrity of Nepal.
7. Parties are expected to hold internal election for its office bearers every 5 years.
8. The party should ensure certain levels of representation for minority and under-represented groups among its election candidates.
9. The source of income of the proposed political party and details of such sources.
10. There should be the provision for inclusiveness of members from neglected and suppressed regions including Women and Dalits, in the executive committee.
11. The Constitution of the party should have an effective system of making the members disciplined.
12. The Election Commission shall not register a party if any Nepali citizen is discriminated against on the basis of religion, caste, tribe, language or sex.

13. Parties must have a flag.
14. The party will not be registered if its name, objectives, insignia or flag is of a nature that would disturb the religious or communal harmony or of the nature to divided the country, or if the party constitution rules are for purposes or protecting and promoting a partyless single party system of governance.
15. A list of signatures of at least 10 thousand voting supporters is to be submitted along with the application for registration of any party outside the parliament.
16. Political parties with objectives contrary to the spirit and norms of the preamble of this constitution shall not be considered qualified for party registration.

Only parties that live up to the conditions are entitled to receive national symbols for their candidates. Parties who do not meet the criteria are disqualified.

APPENDIX - III

List of political parties registered ahead of the 2006 municipal election

S.No.	Party	Party leader
1.	Nepal Conservative Party	Bharat Bahadur Bishural
2.	Samyukta Janashakti Nepal	Dr. Bal Bahadur Khatri Chhetri
3.	Rastriya Jagerna Party	Hari Bahadur Basnet
4.	Nepal Rastriya Loktantrik Dal	Amar KC
5.	Panchayat Prajatantra Party	Bhim Narayan Sharma Poudel
6.	Nepal Shanti Kshetra Parishad	Sushma Sharma Badal
7.	Nepal Party	Lekhnath Poudel
8.	Shiva Sena Nepal	Arun Subedi
9.	Swatantra Nepal Prajatantra Party	Shambhu Gajurel Chhetri
10.	Nepal Rastriya Janakalyan Party	Khushilal Yadav
11.	Nepal Prajaparishad	Ramhari Sharma
12.	Shanti Party Nepal	Jhanak Prasad Dhungana
13.	Social Democratic Party	Shanta Chitrakar
14.	Nepali Rastriya Congress	Naresh Jung Rana
15.	Hariyali Nepal Party	Pushpa Prasad Luitel
16.	Samyukta Prajatantra Party, Nepal	K. B. Shahi
17.	Nepal Janabhawana Party	Surya Bahadur Khadka 'Vikharchi'
18.	Nepal Shadbhawana Party	Badri Prasad Mandal
19.	Samajbadi Party Nepal	Shalim Miya Ansari
20.	Jana Congress	Manoj Prasad Lakaul
21.	Nepal Gorkha Rastriya Mukti Morcha	Nagendra Tamang
22.	Rastriya Prajantra Party	Pashupati Shumsher JB Rana
23.	Pragatishil Upayog Tatoa Nepal	Yagya Prasad Bastola
24.	Dalit Majdoor Kishan Party	Bimal Prasad Yadav
25.	Rastriya Janamukti Party	Makwar Singh Thapa
26.	Nepal Socialist Party	Kunwar Kanta
27.	Muskan Sena Nepal	Muskan Poudel
28.	Dalit Janajati Party	Biswendra Pashwan
29.	Rastriya Janarajya Parishad	Manikraj Bajracharya
30.	Samajbadi Gareeb Party	Ashok Kumar Jha
31.	Nepali Congress (Subarna)	Pralhad Humagai
32.	Akhil Nepal Samata Party	Ram Chandra Shah Teli
33.	National Socialist Party	Jagan Bahadur Rai Kirant

34.	Nepali Janata Dal	Ram Dulari Devi Shah
35.	Supremacy of Nepalis People	Khyam Narayan Shah
36.	Rastriya Jana Ekta Party	Manmohan Shamsher JB Rana
37.	Rastriya Janashakti Party	Surya Bahadur Thapa
38.	Nepal Deshbahkta Party	Basanta Jung Bahadur Singh
39.	Rastriya Jana Prajatantrik Party	Kameshor Singh Subedi
40.	Janata Dal (Samajbadi Prajatantrik)	Dr. Kesharjung Rayamajhi
41.	Nepali Dalit Shramik Morcha	Kailashman BK
42.	Nepal Samata Party	Narayan Singh Pun
43.	Rastriya Janata Party, Nepal	Jaya Prakash
44.	Mechi Mahakali Jana Samanwaya Dal	Hit Bahadur Pyakurel
45.	Bahujan Samaj Party Nepal	Pemba Lama
46.	Rashtriya Prajatantra Party (Rastrabadi)	Rajeshwar Devkota
47.	Nepal Jana Prajatantrik Party	Sher Bahadur Karki
48.	Rashtra Bachau Nepal (Save the Nation Nepal)	Prachanda Lal Shrestha
49.	Rastriya Jana Jagaran Party (Manavtabad)	Ashok Lal Shrestha
50.	Rastrabadi Prajatantrik Parishad	Shivabhakta Bhatt
51.	Nepal Swatantra Samajbadi Party Sahara (Rana)	Sagar
52.	Nepal Rastriya Ekta Party	Daya Krishna Neupane
53.	Rastrabadi Milan Kendra Nepal	Ganesh Bahadur Pandey
54.	Rastrabadi Yuba Morcha	Shyam Kumar Thapa
55.	Nepal Samata Party (Samajbadi)	Dayananda Thapa
56.	Nepal Deshbhakta Prajatantrik Party	Prakash Gurung
57.	Janamukti Party Nepal	Atalman Rai
58.	Nepal Rastriya Jana Bhawana Party	Bhim Bahadur Tamang
59.	Rastrabadi Janta	Dal Yunush Anshari
60.	Rastrabadi Ekta Party	Uma Shrestha (Hima)
61.	Prajatantrik Janamukti Party	Gore Bahadur Khapangi
62.	Rastriya Bikash Party	Dr. Asharphi Shah
63.	Nepal Co-operative Party	Toyanath Dahal
64.	Prajatantrik Nepal	Keshar Bahadur Bista
65.	Samajbadi Prajatantrik Janata Party Nepal	Prem Bahadur Singh
66.	Bir Nepali Prajatantrik Party	Bir Bahadur Gurung
67.	Nepal Gyanshil Party	Damber Narayan Yadav

68.	Shanti Ekta Rastriya Dal	Karma Bahdur Singh (Thakuri)
69.	Nepali Congress (Rastrabadi)	Dr. Durga Pokharel
70.	Liberal Samajbadi Party Nepal	Baburam Dhakal Shastri
71.	Nepal Manav Adhikar Tatha Samaj Kalian Party	Uddhav Prasad Gautam
72.	Rastriya Jansewa Dal	Ram Lal Shrestha

APPENDIX – IV

List of Political Parties Registered with the Election Commission at the time of CA Election

S.No.	*Name of the Political Parties*	*Election Symbols*	
1	Communist Party of Nepal (Unified – Marxist – Leninist)	Sun	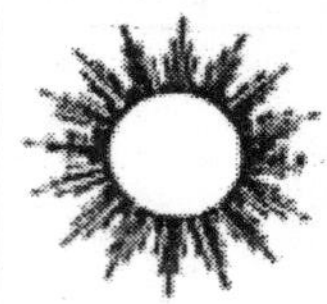
2	Nepali Congress	Tree	
3	Rastriya Janasshakti Party	Umbrella	
4	Rastriya Prajatantra Party	Plough	
5	Janamorcha Nepal	Pentagonal Star	
6	Nepal Communist Party (Maoist)	Hammer and Sickle inside a circle	
7	Nepal Majdoor Kisan Party (Nepal Workers and Peasants Party)	Madal (Drum)	

8	Samajbadi Prajatantrik Party Nepal (Sccialist Democratic Party Nepal)	Half Moon	
9	Rastriya Janmorcha	Glass	
10	Nepal Rastriya Bikas Party	Radio	
11	Samajbadi Party Nepal	Bicycle	
12	Rastriya Janamukti Party	House	
13	Rastriya Prajatantra Party Nepal	Cow	
14	Nepal Communist Party Eki-krit (Integrated)	Oil-fed lamp	
15	Nepal Communist Party (Marxist-Leninist)	Sickle and Star	

16	Rastriya Janata Dal	Ball	
17	Nepal Communist Party Samyukta (United)	Sickle	
18	Nepal Samata Party	Fish	
19	Dalit Janjati Party	Water Jug	
20	Nepal Shadvawana Party (Ananda Devi)	Palm	
21	Hariyali Nepal Party	Mango	
22	Nepal Communist Party Samyukta Marxbadi (United Marxist)	Trident	
23	Shivasena Nepal	Damaru	
24	Madhesi Janaadhikar Forum Nepal	Light in Hand	

25	Nepal Cooperative Party	Pen and Copy	
26	Nepal Communist Party (Marxist)	Spade	
27	Hindu Prajatantrik Party	Lady	
28	Nawa Janabadi Morcha	Baby	
29	Nepal Rastriya Janakalyan Party	Two Eyes	
30	Rastrabadi Milan Kendra Nepal Dal	Rose	
31	Rastriya Bikas Party	Elephant	
32	Nepal Communist Party (Marxist-Leninist-Maoist Center)	Ear of Corn	

33	Muskan Sena Nepal Party	Man	
34	Leeg Nepal Shanti Ekata Party	Horse	
35	Nepali Janatantra Party	Axe	
36	Rastriya Jana Ekata Party	Bulb	
37	Nepal Jansangh Party	Peacock	
38	Prajatantrik Shakti Party	Watch	
39	Nepal Janabhavana Party	Oil-fed Lamp Stand	
40	Rastriya Jan Prajatantrik Party	Rhino	

41	Nepal Shanti Chhetra Parishad	A Pair of Hands	
42	Rastrabadi Yuba Morcha	Spectacle	
43	Nepali Rastriya Janabhawana Party	Tea Kettle	
44	Liberal Samajbadi Party (Liberal Democratic Party)	Tiger	
45	Prajatantrik Shanti Party	Cob of Rice	
46	Nepali Janata Dal	Wheel	
47	Nepal Rastriya Loktantrik Dal	Cap	
48	Rastrabadi Ekata Party	Pigeon	

49	Nepali Congress (Rastrabadi)	Faucet	
50	Prajatantrik Janamukti Party	Comb	
51	Janamukti Party Nepal	Ladder	
52	Loktantrik Janata Party Nepal	Aeroplane	
53	Nepal Jagriti Dal	A Child in the lap of mother	
54	Shasakti Nepal	Weighing machine	
55	Rastriya Janata Dal Nepal	Lantern	
56	Nepal Prajatantrik Yuba Party	Cross-Khukuri	

57	Shanti Party Nepal	Hexagon (Shadkon)	
58	Nepal Janata party	Lotus Flower	
59	Nepal Bahudal Party	Temple	
60	Lok Kalaynkari Janata Party Nepal	Bow and Arrow	
61	Shadbhavana Party	Arrow	
62	Tarai-Madesh Loktantrik Party	A pair of bulls	
63	Mongol National Organization	Rooster	
64	Nepal Samyabadi Dal	Jug (Karuwa)	
65	Nepal Pariwar Dal	Key	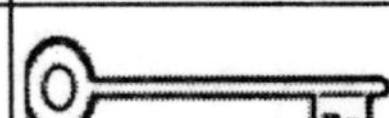
66	Sanghiya Loktantrik Rastriay Manch	Khukuri inside a sheave	

67	Nepa Rastriya Party	Scimitar	
68	Madhesi – Janadhikar Forum	Weaving Machine	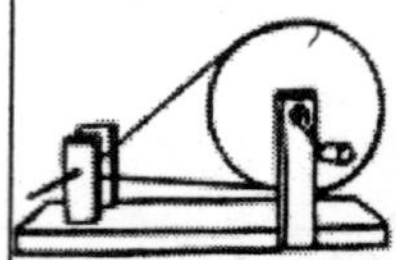
69	Nepal – Loktantrik Samajbadi Dal	Pen	
70	Nepal Sukumbashi Party (Loktantrik)	Bamboo Basket	
71	Nepali Dalit Shramik Morcha	Kite	
72	Churebhavar Rastriya Ekata Party Nepal	Boomerang Ring	
73	Tamsaling Nepal Rastriya Dal	Trumpet	
74	Nawa Nepal Prajatantrik Dal	Bell	

APPENDIX – V

Sl. No.	Task description	15 Jan – 12 Feb				13 Feb – 13 Mar				14 Mar – 12 Apr				13-26 Apr	
		1	2	3	4	1	2	3	4	1	2	3	4	1	2
1.	Registration of Political parties														
2.	Preparation, production and transportation of voter education materials														
3.	Development and production of VE materials and Launching of Campaign														
4.	VE volunteer training and mobilization														
5.	Decision on polling centres														
6.	Implementation and monitoring of the Election Code of Conduct														
7.	Purchasing, printing, packing and transporting electoral materials														
8.	Preparation of details of staff to be deployed for poll management														
9.	Appointment of and training for returning officers and setting up officer														
10.	Electoral programme relating to (party) candidates contesting the PR race														

11.	Conducting the electoral programme under FPTP														
12.	Training for polling and vote counting staff														
13.	Orientation for political parties and civil society														
14.	Development of election result-related software and training on its use														
15.	Electoral observer management														
16.	Media monitoring														
17.	Setting up and operating media centre														
18.	Designing, printing and transporting ballot papers														
19.	Polling (10 April 2008)														
20	Vote counting and result processing														

APPENDIX - VI

Parties and Candidates

SL. No.	*Political Party*	*No. of candidates for FPTP*	*No. of candidates for PR*	*Top candidate*
1	Chure Bhawar Rastriya Ekta Party Nepal	11	43	Keshav Prasad Mainali
2	Communist Party of Nepal (Maoist)	240	335	Lila Devi Mehta
3	Communist Party of Nepal (Marxist)	4	38	Durga Prasad Gyawali
4	Communist Party of Nepal (Marxist-Leninist)	113	138	C.P. Mainali
5	Communist Party of Nepal (Unified Marxist-Leninist)	240	335	Amrit Bohara
6	Communist Party of Nepal (Unified)	136	335	Bishnu Bahadur Ta-mang
7	Communist Party of Nepal (United Marxist)	48	100	Hemanta Bahadur B.C.
8	Communist Party of Nepal (United)	55	67	Chandra Dev Joshi
9	Dalit Janajati Party	50	74	Biswendra Paswan
10	Hindu Prajatantrik Party	4	64	Bisnhu Kumar Prasai
11	Janamorcha Nepal	203	335	Ritakumari Sunar
12	Janamukti Party Nepal	3	79	Lakshmi Devi Tuladhar

13	Liberal Samajbadi Party	3		
14	League Nepal Shanti Ekta Party	10	63	Sharan Bahadur Bhandari
15	Lok Kalayankari Janata Party Nepal	34	100	Kishori Mehta
16	Madhesi Janaadhikar Forum, Nepal	103	100	Ramjanam Chaudhuri
17	Mongol National Organisation	17	46	Krishna Bahadur Tamang
18	Muskan Sena Nepal Party	34	46	Pradip Giri
19	Nawa Janabadi Morcha	15	38	Shankarlal Shrestha
20	Nawa Nepal Prajatantrik Dal	2	36	Anoop Kumar Pahari
21	Nepal Rastriya Party	6	73	Buddharatna Manandhar
22	Nepal Dalit Shramik Morcha	1	46	Roma Bishwakarma
23	Nepal Janabhavana Party	2	49	Ram Kishun Pasi
24	Nepal Janata Party	25	58	Khemnath Acharya
25	Nepal Loktantrik Samajbadi Dal	11	84	Tara Chandra Chauduri
26	Nepal Rastriya Bikas Party	13	42	Takashi Miyahara
27	Nepal Rastriya Janakalayan Party	3		
28	Nepal Rastriya Loktantrik Dal	2	36	Binod Kumar Kshetri
29	Nepal Sadhabhavana Party (Anandidevi)	104	76	Rakesh Kumar Gupta

30	Nepal Samata Party	14	35	Sakila Ranjitkar
31	Nepal Samyabadi Dal	1	42	Mukunda Khanal
32	Nepal Shanti Kshetra Parishad	3	40	Tilakbahadur Negi
33	Nepal Sukumbasi Party (Loktantrik)	11	58	Manju Kumari Suyal
34	Nepal Workers & Peasants Party	98	86	Prem Suval
35	Nepali Congress	240	335	G.P. Koirala
36	Nepali Congress (Rastrabadi)	0	50	Khanuparude
37	Nepali Janata Dal	40	99	Bishwanath Prasad Agrawal
38	Rashtrabadi Ekta Party	2	50	Chandra Maya Maha-rjan
39	Rashtrabadi Yuba Morcha	5	59	Shyam Kumar Thapa
40	Rastriya Bikas Party	21	38	Asarfi Shah
41	Rastriya Janamorcha	122	335	Santbahadur Nepali
42	Rastriya Janamukti Party	84	100	Urmila Kumari Nepali
43	Rastriya Janata Dal	8	39	Bhogendra Nath Shah Kanu
44	Rastriya Janata Dal Nepal	17	81	Bharat Prasad Mehta
45	Rastriya Janshakti Party	198	304	Shakuntala Devi
46	Rastriya Prajatantra Party	233	335	Lokendra Bahadur Chand

47	Rastriya Prajatantra Party Nepal	204	266	Bhojraj Ghimire
48	Sadbhavana Party	87	100	Bishwanath Singh Rajbanshi
49	Samajbadi Party Nepal	5	41	Mumtaz Alam
50	Samajbadi Prajatantrik Janata Party, Nepal	50	175	Prem Bahadur Singh
51	Sanghiya Loktantrik Rastriya Manch	45	100	Dev Kumar Buddhist
52	Sa-Shakti Nepal	6	64	Padmani Pradhan
53	Shanti Party Nepal	12	69	Tej Prasad Upadhaya
54	Tamsaling Nepal Rastriya Dal	22	54	Parshuram Tamang
55	Tarai-Madhesh Loktantrik Party	94	100	Mahendra Prasad Yadav
56	Independents	816		

APPENDIX - VII

Election Performance of Political Parties

Party	FPTP			Proportional		Seats				
	Votes	%	+/–%—	Votes	%	FPTP	Prop.	Nomi-nated	Total	%
Communist Party of Nepal (Maoist)	3,145,519	30.52		3,144,204	29.28	120	100		220	36.60
Nepali Congress	2,348,890	22.79	–14.50	2,269,883	21.14	37	73		110	18.30
Communist Party of Nepal (Unified Marx-ist-Leninist)	2,229,064	21.63	–16.62	2,183,370	20.33	33	70		103	17.14
Madhesi Jana adhikar Forum, Nepal	634,154	6.15		678,327	6.32	30	22		52	8.65
Tarai-Madhesh Loktantrik Party	345,587	3.35		338,930	3.16	9	11		20	3.33
Rastriya Praja-tantra Party	310,214	3.01	–10.84	263,431	2.45	0	8		8	1.33
Communist Party of Nepal (Marxist-Lenin-ist)	168,196	1.63		243,545	2.27	0	8		8	1.33

Sadbhavana Party	174,086	1.69		167,517	1.56	4	5		9	1.50
Janamorcha Nepal	136,846	1.33	–0.89	164,381	1.53	2	5		7	1.16
Communist Party of Nepal (United)	39,100	0.38		154,968	1.44	0	5		5	0.83
Rastriya Prajatantra Party Nepal	76,684	0.74		110,519	1.03	0	4		4	0.50
Rastriya Janamorcha	93,578	0.91		106,224	0.99	1	3		4	0.66
Rastriya Janshakti Party	79,925	0.77		102,147	0.95	0	3		3	0.50
Nepal Workers Peasants Party	65,908	0.64	+0.08	74,089	0.69	2	2		4	0.66
Sanghiya Loktantrik Rastriya Manch	36,060	0.35		71,958	0.67	0	2		2	0.33
Nepal Sadbhavana Party (Anandidevi)	45,254	0.44	–2.78	55,671	0.52	0	2		2	0.33
Rastriya Janamukti Party	38,568	0.37	–0.70	53,910	0.50	0	2		2	0.33

Nepali Janata Dal	17,162	0.17	+0.04	48,990	0.46	0	2		2	0.33
Communist Party of Nepal (Unified)	51,928	0.50		48,600	0.45	0	2		2	0.33
Dalit Janajati Party	31,444	0.30		40,348	0.37	0	1		1	0.17
Nepa Rastriya Party	11,352	0.11		37,757	0.35	0	1		1	0.17
Samajbadi Prajatantrik Janata Party	13,246	0.13		35,752	0.33	0	1		1	0.17
Chure Bhawar Rastriya Ekta Party	18,908	0.13		28,575	0.27	0	1		1	0.17
Nepal Loktantrik Samajbadi Dal	10,432	0.10		25,022	0.23	0	1		1	0.17
Nepal Parivar Dal	—			23,512	0.22	—	1		1	0.17
Communist Party of Nepal (Marxist)	1,759	0.02		21,234	0.20	0	0		0	
Tamsaling Nepal Rastriya Dal	5,468	0.05		20,657	0.19	0	0		0	

Rastriya Janata Dal	5,556	0.05		19,305	0.18	0	0		0	
Communist Party of Nepal (United Marxist)	10,076	0.10	–0.04	18,717	0.17	0	0		0	
Lok Kalayankari Janata Party	6,700	0.06		18,123	0.17	0	0		0	
Nepal Janabha-vana Party	104	0.00	±0.00	13,173	0.12	0	0		0	
Rastriya Janata Dal Nepal	4,497	0.04		12,678	0.12	0	0		0	
Nepal Janata Party	5,635	0.05		12,531	0.12	0	0		0	
Mongol National Organisation	6,349	0.06	–0.01	11,578	0.11	0	0		0	
Nepal Shanti Kshetra Parishad	45	0.00		10,565	0.10	0	0		0	
Shanti Party Nepal	970	0.01		10,511	0.10	0	0		0	
Rastriya Bikas Party	2,612	0.02		9,329	0.09	0	0		0	

Nepal Sukumbasi Party (Loktantrik)	1,459	0.01		8,322	0.08	0	0		0	
Nepal Rastriya Bikas Party	1,603	0.01		8,026	0.07	0	0		0	
Nepal Dalit Shramik Morcha	93	0.00	–0.08	7,107	0.07	0	0		0	
Samajbadi Party Nepal	1,197	0.01		6,564	0.06	0	0		0	
Muskan Sena Nepal Party	2,490	0.02		6,292	0.06	0	0		0	
Nepali Congress (Rastrabadi)		—		5,721	0.05	—	0		0	
Nepal Samyabadi Dal	60	0.00		5,478	0.05	0	0		0	
Nawa Janabadi Morcha	992	0.01		5,193	0.05	0	0		0	
Hindu Prajatantrik Party	265	0.00		4,902	0.05	0	0		0	
Nepal Samata Party	459	0.00		4,697	0.04	0	0		0	
Rastrabadi Yuba Morcha	496	0.00		4,772	0.04	0	0		0	
League Nepal Shanti Ekta Party	316	0.00		4,443	0.04	0	0		0	

Rastrabadi Ekta Party	43	0.00		4,150	0.04	0	0		0	
Sa-Shakti Nepal	532	0.00		3,752	0.03	0	0		0	
Janamukti Party Nepal	281	0.00	–0.11	3,396	0.03	0	0		0	
Nepal Rastriya Loktantrik Dal	57	0.00		3,216	0.03	0	0		0	
Nawa Nepal Prajatantrik Dal	34	0.00		3,016	0.03	0	0		0	
Liberal Samajbadi Party	152	0.00		—		0	—		0	
Nepal Rastriya Janakalayan Party	96	0.00		—		0	—		0	
Independents	123,619	1.20	–1.54	—		2	—		2	0.33
Not yet determined	—							26	26	—
Total (turn-out %)	10,306,120	100.00	—	10,739,078	100.00	240	335	26	**601**	100.00
Source: www.election.gov.np nepalnews.com										

APPENDIX - VIII

List of Winning Candidates

S.No	*District*	*Cont.*	*Candidate Name*	*Party Name*	*Gen*	*Age*	*E.City*	*Total Votes*
1	Taplejung	1	Surya Man Gurung	Nepali Congress	M	64	Janajati	8719
2	Taplejung	2	Damber Dhoj Tum-bahamphe	Communist Party of Nepal (UML)	M	50	Janajati	8628
3	Paanchthar	1	Purna Kumar Serma	Nepali Congress	M	64	Janajati	12920
4	Paanchthar	2	Damber Singh Sambahamphe	Communist Party of Nepal (UML)	M	45	Janajati	12402
5	Ilam	1	Jhal Nath Khanal	Communist Party of Nepal (UML)	M	58	Bahun	17655
6	Ilam	2	Subash Nembang	Communist Party of Nepal (UML)	M	55	Janajati	17748
7	Ilam	3	Kul Bahadur Gurung	Nepali Congress	M	73	Janajati	16286
8	Jhapa	1	Dharma Prasad Ghimire	Communist Party of Nepal (Maoist)	M	62	Bahun	15276

9	Jhapa	2	Gauri Shankar Khadka	Communist Party of Nepal (Maoist)	M	47	Chhetri	18580
10	Jhapa	3	Purna Prasad Rajbansi	Communist Party of Nepal (Maoist)	M	43	Janajati	16685
11	Jhapa	4	Dharma Sila Chap-again	Communist Party of Nepal (Maoist)	F	35	Bahun	19289
12	Jhapa	5	Keshav Kumar Budhathoki	Nepali Congress	M	64		16466
13	Jhapa	6	Dipak Karki	Communist Party of Nepal (UML)	M	47	Chhetri	14196
14	Jhapa	7	Bishwodip Ling-den Limbu	Communist Party of Nepal (Maoist)	M	32	Janajati	16099
15	Sankhuwasabha	1	Purna Prasad Rai	Communist Party of Nepal (Maoist)	M	43	Janajati	12948
16	Sankhuwasabha	2	Dambar Bahadur Khadka	Communist Party of Nepal (UML)	M	42	Chhetri	10870
17	Tehrathum	1	Tulsi Subba	Nepali Congress	M	52	Janajati	19113

18	Bhojpur	1	Padam Bahadur Rai	Communist Party of Nepal (Maoist)	M	41	Janajati	15796
19	Bhojpur	2	Sudan Rai	Communist Party of Nepal (Maoist)	M	29	Janajati	17578
20	Dhankuta	1	Hem Raj Bhandari	Communist Party of Nepal (Maoist)	M	32	Bahun	17202
21	Dhankuta	2	Hari Raj Limbu	Communist Party of Nepal (Maoist)	M	39	Janajati	12299
22	Morang	1	Amod Prasad Updhaya	Nepali Congress	M	72	Bahun	11105
23	Morang	2	Lal Bahadur Su-sling Magar	Communist Party of Nepal (Maoist)	M	37	Janajati	16567
24	Morang	3	Sabitri Kumar Kafle	Communist Party of Nepal (Maoist)	M	43	Bahun	15863
25	Morang	4	Rama Nand Mandal	Madhesi People's Rights Forum, Nepal	M	43	Madhesi	9894
26	Morang	5	Upendra Yadav	Madhesi People's Rights Forum, Nepal	M	48	Madhesi	27508

27	Morang	6	Bhim Raj Chaud-hari Rajbansi	Madhesi People's Rights Forum, Nepal	M	57	Janjati	17086
28	Morang	7	Bijaya Kumar Gachchhadar	Madhesi People's Rights Forum, Nepal	M	53	Janjati	18416
29	Morang	8	Gopi Nahadur Sarki (Achhami)	Communist Party of Nepal (Maoist)	M	33	Dalit	14375
30	Morang	9	Narendra Bahadur Dhimal	Communist Party of Nepal (M)	M	47	Janjati	14930
31	Sunsari	1	Kiran Kumar Rai	Communist Party of Nepal (Maoist)	M	32	Janjati	18620
32	Sunsari	2	Dharma Raj Ni-raula	Communist Party of Nepal (UML)	M	50	Bahun	15636
33	Sunsari	3	Bijaya Kumar Gachchhadar	Madhesi People's Rights Forum, Nepal	M	53	Janjati	23769
34	Sunsari	4	Muga Lal Mahato	Madhesi People's Rights Forum, Nepal	M	66	Madhesi	19945
35	Sunsari	5	Upendra Yadav	Madhesi People's Rights Forum, Nepal	M	48	Madhesi	23939

36	Sunsari	6	Bhim Prasad Acharya	Communist Party of Nepal (UML)	M	47	Bahun	15664
37	Solukhumbu	1	Gopal Kirati	Communist Party of Nepal (Maoist)	M	42	Janjati	19095
38	Khotang	1	Ram Kumar Rai	Communist Party of Nepal (Maoist)	M	39	Janjati	16687
39	Khotang	2	Samita Karki	Communist Party of Nepal (Maoist)	F	28	Chhetri	18168
40	Okhaldhunga	1	Keshav Rai	Communist Party of Nepal (Maoist)	M	36	Janjati	11635
41	Okhaldhunga	2	Bal Krishna Dhun-gel	Communist Party of Nepal (Maoist)	M	38	Bahun	11069
42	Udaypur	1	Narayan Khadka	Nepali Congress	M	55	Chhetri	14468
43	Udaypur	2	Mani Khambu Kirati	Communist Party of Nepal (Maoist)	F	28	Janjati	13598
44	Udaypur	3	Mohan Bahadur Khatri	Communist Party of Nepal (Maoist)	M	32	Chhetri	14775

45	Saptari	1	Hem Raj Tated	Madhesi People's Rights Forum, Nepal	M	48	Madhesi	9879
46	Saptari	2	Jaya Prakash Gupta	Madhesi People's Rights Forum, Nepal	M	47	Madhesi	8515
47	Saptari	3	Mahesh Prasad Yadav	Sadhvawana Party	M	37	Madhesi	10302
48	Saptari	4	Renu Kumari Yadav	Madhesi People's Rights Forum, Nepal	F	39	Madhesi	12681
49	Saptari	5	Sadrul Miya Haq	Independent	M	49	Madhesi	10603
50	Saptari	6	Mrigendra Kumar Singh Yadav	Madhesi People's Rights Forum, Nepal	M	49	Madhesi	14028
51	Siraha	1	Laxman Mahato	Madhesi People's Rights Forum, Nepal	M	57	Madhesi	9814
52	Siraha	2	Raj Lal Yadav	Madhesi People's Rights Forum, Nepal	M	62	Madhesi	16684
53	Siraha	3	Bijaya Kumar Yadav	Madhesi People's Rights Forum, Nepal	M	?	Madhesi	14884

54	Siraha	4	Shatrughan Prasad Singh Koiree	Madhesi People's Rights Forum, Nepal	M	?	Madhesi	11779
55	Siraha	5	Mahendra Paswan	Communist Party of Nepal (Maoist)	M	64	Dalit	12110
56	Siraha	6	Raj Kishwor Yadav	Madhesi People's Rights Forum, Nepal	M	34	Madhesi	15551
57	Dolakha	1	Devi Khadka	Communist Party of Nepal (Maoist)	F	28	Chhetri	22182
58	Dolakha	2	Hem Bahadur Shrestha	Communist Party of Nepal (Maoist)	M	38	Janjati	18793
59	Ramechhap	1	Tara Narayan Shrestha	Communist Party of Nepal (Maoist)	M	35	Janjati	19910
60	Ramechhap	2	Dilliman Tamang	Communist Party of Nepal (Maoist)	M	35	Janjati	31121
61	Sindhuli	1	Bisham Lal Adhi-kari	Communist Party of Nepal (UML)	M	40	Janjati	12058
62	Sindhuli	2	Chandra Prasad Gajurel	Communist Party of Nepal (Maoist)	M	60	Bahun	18398

63	Sindhuli	3	Neer Kumari Kunwar	Communist Party of Nepal (Maoist)	F	38	Janjati	14944
64	Dhanusha	1	Ram Chandra Jha	Communist Party of Nepal (UML)	M	51	Madhesi	12183
65	Dhanusha	2	Ram Krishna Yadav	Nepali Congress	M	46	Madhesi	9825
66	Dhanusha	3	Bimalendra Nidhi	Nepali Congress	M	50	Madhesi	15582
67	Dhanusha	4	Sanjay Kumar Shah	Madhesi People's Rights Forum, Nepal	M	31	Madhesi	13422
68	Dhanusha	5	Ram Baran Yadav	Nepali Congress	M	62	Madhesi	10392
69	Dhanusha	6	Ram Kumari Devi Yadav	Communist Party of Nepal (Maoist)	F	53	Madhesi	11570
70	Dhanusha	7	Shatrudhan Ma-hato	Communist Party of Nepal (UML)	M	37	Madhesi	11620
71	Mahottari	1	Gireeraj Mani Pokhrel	Janamorcha Nepal	M	51	Bahun	10196
72	Mahottari	2	Hari Narayan Yadav	Madhesi People's Rights Forum, Nepal	M	43	Madhesi	7457

73	Mahottari	3	Ganesh Tiwari Nepali	Tarai Madhes Loktantrik Party	M	65		11390
74	Mahottari	4	RamKumar Sharma	Tarai Madhes Loktantrik Party	M	37	Bahun	9564
75	Mahottari	5	Kaushal Kumar Raya Yadav	Madhesi People's Rights Forum, Nepal	M	36	Madhesi	8609
76	Mahottari	6	Sharad Singh Bhandari	Madhesi People's Rights Forum, Nepal	M	50	Bahun	6862
77	Sarlahi	1	Prakesh Pakhrin	Communist Party of Nepal (UML)	M	49	Janjati	12726
78	Sarlahi	2	Muhamad Rijwan Ansari	Communist Party of Nepal (UML)	M	40	Madhesi	9156
79	Sarlahi	3	Sumitra Devi Raya Yadav	Tarai Madhes Loktantrik Party	F	47	Madhesi	11868
80	Sarlahi	4	Rajendra Mahato	Sadhvawana Party	M	49	Madhesi	17073
81	Sarlahi	5	Khobhari Raya	Sadhvawana Party	M	42	Madhesi	13142
82	Sarlahi	6	Shiva Pujan Raya Yadav	Madhesi People's Rights Forum, Nepal	M	38	Madhesi	15688

83	Rasuwa	1	Prem Bahadur Tamang	Communist Party of Nepal (Maoist)	M	32	Janjati	11147
84	Dhading	1	Puspa Bikram Malla	Communist Party of Nepal (Maoist)	M	54	Janjati	29555
85	Dhading	2	Kalpana Dhamala	Communist Party of Nepal (Maoist)	F	33	Chhetri	20730
86	Dhading	3	Shalik Ram Jamar-kattel	Communist Party of Nepal (Maoist)	M	36		25075
87	Nuwakot	1	Bimala Subedi	Communist Party of Nepal (Maoist)	F	28	Bahun	20581
88	Nuwakot	2	Dr. Ramsharan Mahat	Nepali Congress	M	56	Chhetri	17442
89	Nuwakot	3	Posta Bahadur Bogati	Communist Party of Nepal (Maoist)	M	56	Chhetri	16735
90	Kathmandu	1	Prakash Man Singh	Nepali Congress	M	52	Janjati	14318
91	Kathmandu	2	Jhakku Prasad Subedi	Communist Party of Nepal (Maoist)	M	47	Bahun	13858
92	Kathmandu	3	Chakra Bahadur Thakuri	Nepali Congress	M	50	Chhetri	12966

93	Kathmandu	4	Suprabha Ghimire	Nepali Congress	F	66	Bahun	13451
94	Kathmandu	5	Narahari Acharya	Nepali Congress	M	54	Bahun	13245
95	Kathmandu	6	Hit Man Shakya	Communist Party of Nepal (Maoist)	M	44	Janjati	10768
96	Kathmandu	7	Hisila Yami (Bhattarai)	Communist Party of Nepal (Maoist)	F	48	Janjati	12276
97	Kathmandu	8	Nabindra Raj Joshi	Nepali Congress	M	41	Bahun	11005
98	Kathmandu	9	Dhyan Gobinda Ranjit	Nepali Congress	M	62	Janjati	12501
99	Kathmandu	10	Pushpa Kamal Dahal (Prachanda)	Communist Party of Nepal (Maoist)	M	52	Bahun	23277
100	Bhaktapur	1	Narayanman Bijukchhe	Nepal Workers and Peasants Party	M	67	Janjati	19972
101	Bhaktapur	2	Sunil Prajapati	Nepal Workers and Peasants Party	M	42	Janjati	18100
102	Lalitpur	1	Barsha Man Pun Magar	Communist Party of Nepal (Maoist)	M	36	Janjati	15329

103	Lalitpur	2	Raj Kaji Maharjan	Communist Party of Nepal (Maoist)	M	29	Janjati	17088
104	Lalitpur	3	Pampha Bhushal	Communist Party of Nepal (Maoist)	F	45	Bahun	18930
105	Kavrepalanchok	1	Suryaman Dong Tamang	Communist Party of Nepal (Maoist)	M	37	Janjati	27471
106	Kavrepalanchok	2	Akal Bahadur Thing	Communist Party of Nepal (Maoist)	M	37	Janjati	18207
107	Kavrepalanchok	3	Krishna Prasad Sapkota	Communist Party of Nepal (UML)	M	54	Bahun	16594
108	Kavrepalanchok	4	Tej Bahadur Mijar	Communist Party of Nepal (Maoist)	M	46	Dalit	22076
109	Sindhupalchok	1	Raj Kumar Shres-tha	Communist Party of Nepal (Maoist)	M	32	Janjati	21320
110	Sindhupalchok	2	Agni Prasad Sap-kota	Communist Party of Nepal (Maoist)	M	50	Bahun	30175
111	Sindhupalchok	3	Dawa Tamang	Communist Party of Nepal (Maoist)	M	34	Janjati	14216

112	Makwanpur	1	Dil Bahadur Ghising	Communist Party of Nepal (Maoist)	M	36	Janjati	21027
113	Makwanpur	2	Prem Bahadur Pulami	Communist Party of Nepal (Maoist)	M	35	Janjati	16976
114	Makwanpur	3	Prahlad Lamichhane	Communist Party of Nepal (Maoist)	M	36	Bahun	18514
115	Makwanpur	4	Kumari Moktan	Communist Party of Nepal (Maoist)	F	28	Janjati	14020
116	Rautahat	1	Baban Singh	Independent	M	31	Madhesi	9201
117	Rautahat	2	Mo. Aftab Alam	Nepali Congress	M	45	Madhesi	16801
118	Rautahat	3	Prabhu Saha Teli	Communist Party of Nepal (Maoist)	M	35	Madhesi	11625
119	Rautahat	4	Krishna Prasad Yadav	Nepali Congress	M	20	Madhesi	9997
120	Rautahat	5	Govinda Chaudhari	Tarai Madhes Loktantrik Party	M	49	Janjati	11732
121	Rautahat	6	Devendra Prasad Patel	Communist Party of Nepal (Maoist)	M	37	Madhesi	10133
122	Bara	1	Saroj Kumar Yadav	Sadhvawana Party	M	34	Madhesi	8182

123	Bara	2	Sivachandra Prasad Kushwaha	Communist Party of Nepal (Maoist)	M	41	Madhesi	10991
124	Bara	3	Pramod Prasad Gupta	Madhesi People's Rights Forum, Nepal	M	29	Madhesi	16081
125	Bara	4	Jitendra Prasad Sonar	Tarai Madhes Loktantrik Party	M	38	Madhesi	9624
126	Bara	5	Uma Kanta Chaud-hari	Nepali Congress	M	39	Janjati	15487
127	Bara	6	Jay Ram Dahal	Communist Party of Nepal (Maoist)	M	35	Bahun	15109
128	Parsa	1	Karima Begam	Madhesi People's Rights Forum, Nepal	F	32	Madhesi	14614
129	Parsa	2	Ajay Kumar Dubedi	Nepali Congress	M	43	Bahun	9531
130	Parsa	3	Ajay Kumar Chau-rasia	Nepali Congress	M	41	Janjati	14650
131	Parsa	4	Pradhumna Prasad Chauhan	Communist Party of Nepal (UML)	M	43	Madhesi	12590
132	Parsa	5	Ramesh Rijal	Nepali Congress	M	51	Bahun	14687

133	Chitwan	1	Lalmani Chaudhari	Communist Party of Nepal (UML)	M	44	Janjati	17971
134	Chitwan	2	Ram Bahadur Thapa	Communist Party of Nepal (Maoist)	M	53	Janjati	21409
135	Chitwan	3	Narayan Prasad Dahal	Communist Party of Nepal (Maoist)	M	52	Bahun	17804
136	Chitwan	4	Chitra Bahadur Shrestha	Communist Party of Nepal (Maoist)	M	54	Janjati	23942
137	Chitwan	5	Amik Sherchan	Janamorcha Nepal	M	64	Janjati	14397
138	Gorkha	1	Parbati Thapa Shrestha	Communist Party of Nepal (Maoist)	F	29	Janjati	40606
139	Gorkha	2	Baburam Bhattrai	Communist Party of Nepal (Maoist)	M	53	Bahun	46272
140	Gorkha	3	Amar Bahadur Gurung (Tamu)	Communist Party of Nepal (Maoist)	M	35	Janjati	28969
141	Manang	1	Dev Prasad Gu-rung	Communist Party of Nepal (Maoist)	M	51	Janjati	1652

142	Lamjung	1	Buddhi Ram Gurung	Communist Party of Nepal (Maoist)	M	37	Janjati	21044
143	Lamjung	2	Prithhivi Subba Gurung	Communist Party of Nepal (UML)	M	50	Janjati	19583
144	Kaski	1	Dev Prasad Gu-rung	Communist Party of Nepal (Maoist)	M	49	Janjati	17409
145	Kaski	2	Raj Kaji Gurung	Communist Party of Nepal (Maoist)	M	30	Janjati	14832
146	Kaski	3	Rabindra Prasad Adhikari	Communist Party of Nepal (UML)	M	39	Bahun	13386
147	Kaski	4	Durga Kumari B.K	Communist Party of Nepal (Maoist)	F	26	Dalit	14866
148	Tanahu	1	Suresh Kumar Ale Magar	Communist Party of Nepal (Maoist)	M	53	Janjati	17744
149	Tanahu	2	Ram Chandra Poudel	Nepali Congress	M	63	Bahun	18970
150	Tanahu	3	Kiran Gurung	Communist Party of Nepal (UML)	M	47	Janjati	14786

151	Syangja	1	Hit Kaji Gurung	Communist Party of Nepal (UML)	M	46	Janjati	18101
152	Syangja	2	Gopal Man Shres-tha	Nepali Congress	M	60	Janjati	17247
153	Syangja	3	Mohan Prasad Pandey	Nepali Congress	M	44	Bahun	18419
154	Gulmi	1	Sudarshan Baral	Communist Party of Nepal (Maoist)	M	31	Bahun	14165
155	Gulmi	2	Pradeep Kumar Gyawli	Communist Party of Nepal (UML)	M	46	Bahun	23253
156	Gulmi	3	Chandra Bahadur Thapa	Communist Party of Nepal (Maoist)	M	33	Janjati	16581
157	Palpa	1	Dal Bahadur Rana	Communist Party of Nepal (UML)	M	47	Janjati	19185
158	Palpa	2	Mrs. Lila Kumari Bagale Somai	Communist Party of Nepal (Maoist)	F	32	Janjati	12750
159	Palpa	3	Kul Prasad Nepal	Communist Party of Nepal (UML)	M	56		12951

160	Arghakhanchi	1	Top Bahadur Ray-amajhi	Communist Party of Nepal (Maoist)	M	46	Chhetri	19584
161	Arghakhanchi	2	Puspa Bhusal	Nepali Congress	F	46	Bahun	16992
162	Nawalparasi	1	Shashanka Koirala	Nepali Congress	M	51	Bahun	17430
163	Nawalparasi	2	Mahendra Dhoj G.C	Nepali Congress	M	50	Chhetri	12166
164	Nawalparasi	3	Sita Devi Boudel	Communist Party of Nepal (Maoist)	F	30	Dalit	13535
165	Nawalparasi	4	Chinak Kurmi	Communist Party of Nepal (Maoist)	M	42	Madhesi	10592
166	Nawalparasi	5	Ram Bachhan Ahir(Yadhav)	Madhesi People's Rights Forum, Nepal	M	51	Madhesi	13641
167	Nawalparasi	6	Hridayesh Tripathi	Tarai Madhes Loktantrik Party	M	48	Madhesi	10029
168	Rupandehi	1	Ghan Shyam Ya-dav Ahir	Communist Party of Nepal (Maoist)	M	38	Madhesi	12624
169	Rupandehi	2	Om Prakash Yadhav	Madhesi People's Rights Forum, Nepal	M	27	Madhesi	10612
170	Rupandehi	3	Bal Krishna Khand	Nepali Congress	M	46	Chhetri	16790

171	Rupandehi	4	Bishnu Prasad Paudel	Communist Party of Nepal (UML)	M	48	Bahun	15880
172	Rupandehi	5	Ramnath Dhakal	Communist Party of Nepal (UML)	M	45	Bahun	11080
173	Rupandehi	6	Omprakash Yadav	Madhesi People's Rights Forum, Nepal	M	33	Madhesi	12170
174	Rupandehi	7	Muhammad Okil Musalman	Madhesi People's Rights Forum, Nepal	M	39	Madhesi	8121
175	Kapilvastu	1	Deep Kumar Upadhaya (Lami-chhane)	Nepali Congress	M	57	Bahun	12997
176	Kapilvastu	2	Dan Bahadur Kurmi	Tarai Madhes Loktantrik Party	M	51	Madhesi	8434
177	Kapilvastu	3	Brijesh Kumar Gupta	Tarai Madhes Loktantrik Party	M	37	Madhesi	18126
178	Kapilvastu	4	Ishwar Dayal Mishra	Tarai Madhes Loktantrik Party	M	40	Madhesi	10394
179	Kapilvastu	5	Abhisek Pratap Shah	Madhesi People's Rights Forum, Nepal	M	25	Chhetri	15694

180	Mustang	1	Chandra Bahadur Garung	Communist Party of Nepal (UML)	M	53	Janjati	2456
181	Myagdi	1	Govinda Paudel	Communist Party of Nepal (Maoist)	M	43	Bahun	23102
182	Baglung	1	Ramjee Prasad Sharma	Communist Party of Nepal (UML)	M	48	Bahun	15786
183	Baglung	2	Chitra Prasad K.C.	Rastriya Janamorcha	M	66	Chhetri	12594
184	Baglung	3	Nara Bahadur Pun	Nepali Congress	M	49	Janjati	11582
185	Parvat	1	Arjun Prasad Joshi	Nepali Congress	M	51	Bahun	13258
186	Parvat	2	Gunakhar Basyal	Communist Party of Nepal (Maoist)	M	30	Bahun	15678
187	Rukum	1	Jun Kumari Roka (Oli)	Communist Party of Nepal (Maoist)	F	30	Janjati	31410
188	Rukum	2	Janardan Sharma	Communist Party of Nepal (Maoist)	M	46	Bahun	30270
189	Rolpa	1	Jaypuri Gharti	Communist Party of Nepal (Maoist)	F	34	Janjati	26505

190	Rolpa	2	Puspa Kamal Dahal (Prachanda)	Communist Party of Nepal (Maoist)	M	52	Bahun	34220
191	Pyuthan	1	Narayan Prasad Adhikari	Communist Party of Nepal (Maoist)	M	44	Bahun	13096
192	Pyuthan	2	Deepak Bahadur K.C.	Communist Party of Nepal (Maoist)	M	65	Chhetri	12857
193	Salyan	1	Tek Bahadur Basnet	Communist Party of Nepal (Maoist)	M	42	Chhetri	27421
194	Salyan	2	Uma Kant Sharma	Communist Party of Nepal (Maoist)	M	46	Bahun	17992
195	Dang	1	Indra Jit Tharu	Communist Party of Nepal (Maoist)	M	28	Janjati	18093
196	Dang	2	Dama Kumari Sharma	Communist Party of Nepal (Maoist)	F	36	Bahun	20240
197	Dang	3	Krishna Bahadur Mahara	Communist Party of Nepal (Maoist)	M	48	Chhetri	20784

198	Dang	4	Shiv Raj Gautam	Communist Party of Nepal (Maoist)	M	69	Bahun	18854
199	Dang	5	Sushma Sharma Ghimire	Communist Party of Nepal (Maoist)	F	41	Bahun	17062
200	Dolpa	1	Ram Bahadur Bohara	Communist Party of Nepal (Maoist)	M	41	Chhetri	9723
201	Mugu	1	Nav Raj Dhami	Communist Party of Nepal (Maoist)	M	38		10100
202	Jumla	1	Naresh Bhandari	Communist Party of Nepal (Maoist)	M	29	Bahun	21127
203	Kalikot	1	Khadga Bahadur Bishwakarma	Communist Party of Nepal (Maoist)	M	39	Dalit	27629
204	Humla	1	Karn Jit Budha-thoki	Communist Party of Nepal (Maoist)	M	36		13318
205	Jajarkot	1	Kali Bahadur Malla	Communist Party of Nepal (Maoist)	M	49		19009

206	Jajarkot	2	Bhakta Bahadur Shah	Communist Party of Nepal (Maoist)	M	45	Chhetri	11938
207	Dailekh	1	Ganesh Bahadur Khadka	Nepali Congress	M	34	Chhetri	16280
208	Dailekh	2	Raj Bahadur Budha	Communist Party of Nepal (UML)	M	41		16292
209	Surkhet	1	Kamala Sharma	Communist Party of Nepal (UML)	F	?	Bahun	18804
210	Surkhet	2	Yam Lal Kandel	Communist Party of Nepal (UML)	M	45	Bahun	16297
211	Surkhet	3	Nara Bahadur Bista	Communist Party of Nepal (Maoist)	M	39	Chhetri	17429
212	Banke	1	Tilak Pariyar	Communist Party of Nepal (Maoist)	M	57	Dalit	16087
213	Banke	2	Mohammad Esti-yak Rai	Madhesi People's Rights Forum, Nepal	M	28	Madhesi	19396
214	Banke	3	Sarbadev Prasad Ojha	Madhesi People's Rights Forum, Nepal	M	48	Bahun	14900

215	Banke	4	Purna Kumari Subedi	Communist Party of Nepal (Maoist)	F	48	Bahun	13884
216	Bardiya	1	Sarala Regmi	Communist Party of Nepal (Maoist)	F	38	Bahun	17955
217	Bardiya	2	Bishnu Prasad Chaudhari Tharu	Communist Party of Nepal (Maoist)	M	35	Janjati	17851
218	Bardiya	3	Sant Kumar Tharu	Communist Party of Nepal (Maoist)	M	41	Janjati	23663
219	Bardiya	4	Ramcharan Chaud-hari (Tharu)	Communist Party of Nepal (Maoist)	M	50	Janjati	24444
220	Bajura	1	Dev Raj Joshi	Nepali Congress	M	44	Bahun	19271
221	Achham	1	Sher Bahadur Kunwar	Communist Party of Nepal (UML)	M	40	Chhetri	21631
222	Achham	2	Sharad Singh Bhandari	Communist Party of Nepal (Maoist)	M	32	Bahun	17976
223	Bajhang	1	Bhanu Bhakta Joshi	Communist Party of Nepal (UML)	M	49	Chhetri	13955

224	Bajhang	2	Shankar Bahadur Khadka	Communist Party of Nepal (Maoist)	M	50	Chhetri	13895
225	Doti	1	Harka Bahadur Singh	Communist Party of Nepal (UML)	M	51	Chhetri	14506
226	Doti	2	Khem Bahadur Bum	Communist Party of Nepal (Maoist)	M	29	Chhetri	10929
227	Kailali	1	Rupa Chaudhari	Communist Party of Nepal (Maoist)	F	29	Janjati	21780
228	Kailali	2	Bhagat Bahadur Baduwal	Communist Party of Nepal (Maoist)	M	36		21219
229	Kailali	3	Bir Man Chaudhari	Communist Party of Nepal (Maoist)	M	34	Janjati	19739
230	Kailali	4	Krishna Kumar Chaudhari	Communist Party of Nepal (Maoist)	M	29	Janjati	27547
231	Kailali	5	Lekh Raj Bhatta	Communist Party of Nepal (Maoist)	M	48	Madhesi	17979

232	Kailali	6	Lila Kumari Bhandari	Communist Party of Nepal (Maoist)	F	31	Bahun	14826
233	Darchula	1	Laxman Dutta Joshi	Communist Party of Nepal (Maoist)	M	30	Bahun	25404
234	Baitadi	1	Narendra Bahadur Kunwar	Communist Party of Nepal (Maoist)	M	37	Chhetri	27130
235	Baitadi	2	Renu Chand (Bhatt)	Communist Party of Nepal (Maoist)	F	27	Madhesi	20021
236	Dadeldhura	1	Sher Bahadur Deuba	Nepali Congress	M	60	Chhetri	20529
237	Kanchanpur	1	Puran Rana Tharu	Communist Party of Nepal (Maoist)	M	26	Janjati	14765
238	Kanchanpur	2	Devi Lal Chaudhari	Communist Party of Nepal (Maoist)	M	31	Janjati	18284
239	Kanchanpur	3	Tekendra Prasad Bhatt	Communist Party of Nepal (Maoist)	M	26	Madhesi	15076
240	Kanchanpur	4	Sher Bahadur Deuba	Nepali Congress	M	60	Chhetri	12824

APPENDIX – IX

CA Members Selected by Proportional Representation

S. No	*Party*	*Name*	*Gender*	*Age*	*Regional Category*	*Castel Elhnic Categ*	*District*
1.	Communist Party of Nepal (Maoist)	Liladevi Mehata	F	31	Madhesi	Janjati	Sunsari
2. 2	Communist Party of Nepal (Maoist)	Jubba Soren	F	31	Madhesi	Others	Morang
3. 3	Communist Party of Nepal (Maoist)	Lalit Kumari Shah	F	28	Madhesi	Others	Saptari
4. 4	Communist Party of Nepal (Maoist)	Sunita Kumari Mahato	F	31	Madhesi	Others	Siraha
5. 5	Communist Party of Nepal (Maoist)	Pramila Devi Yadav	F	38	Madhesi	Others	Dhanusha
6.	Communist Party of Nepal (Maoist)	Budhani Devi Mahato	F	35	Madhesi	Others	Mahottari
7.	Communist Party of Nepal (Maoist)	Jwala Kumari Shah	F	26	Madhesi	Others	Bara
8.	Communist Party of Nepal (Maoist)	Indramati Yadav	F	28	Madhesi	Others	Kapil-vastu

9.	Communist Party of Nepal (Maoist)	Laxmi Kumari Chaud-hary	F	36	Madhesi	Janjati	Saptari
10.	Communist Party of Nepal (Maoist)	Sukdaiya Chaudhary	F	29	Madhesi	Janjati	Kailali
11.	Communist Party of Nepal (Maoist)	Dhruba Aangdambe	M	41	Mountain/ Hills	Janjati	Paanch-thar
12.	Communist Party of Nepal (Maoist)	Shanti Devi Rajbhansi	F	47	Madhesi	Others	Morang
13.	Communist Party of Nepal (Maoist)	Halina Khatoon Shokhin	F	50	Madhesi	Others	Sarlahi
14.	Communist Party of Nepal (Maoist)	Durgi Devi Pasawan	F	35	Madhesi	Dalit	Dhanusha
15.	Communist Party of Nepal (Maoist)	Chanda Devi	F	28	Madhesi	Others	Parsa
16.	Communist Party of Nepal (Maoist)	Siddhartha Somani	M	40	Madhesi	Others	Jhapa
17.	Communist Party of Nepal (Maoist)	Jagat Prasad Yadav	M	30	Madhesi	Others	Siraha
18.	Communist Party of Nepal (Maoist)	Matrika Prasad Yadav	M	49	Madhesi	Others	Dhanusha
19.	Communist Party of Nepal (Maoist)	Shivram Yadav	M	41	Madhesi	Others	Saptari
20.	Communist Party of Nepal (Maoist)	Santosh Tharu	M	26	Madhesi	Janjati	Sunsari

21.	Communist Party of Nepal (Maoist)	Pattu Tharu	M	40	Madhesi	Janjati	Banke
22.	Communist Party of Nepal (Maoist)	Sundara Tharu	M	39	Madhesi	Janjati	Bardiya
23.	Communist Party of Nepal (Maoist)	Bhishma Dhimal	M	57	Madhesi	Janjati	Jhapa
24.	Communist Party of Nepal (Maoist)	Abhi Lal Jhangad	M	54	Madhesi	Others	Morang
25.	Communist Party of Nepal (Maoist)	Babu Lal Paswan	M	55	Madhesi	Dalit	Morang
26.	Communist Party of Nepal (Maoist)	Bharat Prasad Shah	M	35	Madhesi	Others	Mahottari
27.	Communist Party of Nepal (Maoist)	Islam Miya Dhobi	M	52	Madhesi	Others	Parsa
28.	Communist Party of Nepal (Maoist)	Sangh Prasad Tharu	M	38	Madhesi	Janjati	Kapil-vastu
29.	Communist Party of Nepal (Maoist)	Amrita Thapa Magar	F	35	Mountain/ Hills	Janjati	Syangja
30.	Communist Party of Nepal (Maoist)	Tara Gharti Magar	F	32	Mountain/ Hills	Janjati	Rolpa
31.	Communist Party of Nepal (Maoist)	Onsari Gharti Magar	F	30	Mountain/ Hills	Janjati	Rolpa
32.	Communist Party of Nepal (Maoist)	Kamala Rokka	F	32	Mountain/ Hills	Janjati	Rukum

33.	Communist Party of Nepal (Maoist)	Santa Maya Tamang	F	31	Mountain/ Hills	Janjati	Kavrepal-anchok
34.	Communist Party of Nepal (Maoist)	Indrawati Adhikari	F	40	Madhesi	Janjati	Sindhuli
35.	Communist Party of Nepal (Maoist)	Sabitra Gurung Dura	F	30	Mountain/ Hills	Janjati	Tanahu
36.	Communist Party of Nepal (Maoist)	Laxmi Gurung Dura	F	28	Mountain/ Hills	Janjati	Ramech-hap
37.	Communist Party of Nepal (Maoist)	Bishnu Kumari Rai	F	33	Mountain/ Hills	Janjati	Ilam
38.	Communist Party of Nepal (Maoist)	Sushila Kandangwa	F	26	Mountain/ Hills	Janjati	Teh-rathum
39.	Communist Party of Nepal (Maoist)	Anan Dawa Sherpa	F	38	Mountain/ Hills	Janjati	Kath-mandu
40.	Communist Party of Nepal (Maoist)	Maya Chepang	F	35	Mountain/ Hills	Janjati	Chitwan
41.	Communist Party of Nepal (Maoist)	Uma Bhujel	F	30	Mountain/ Hills	Janjati	Gorkha
42.	Communist Party of Nepal (Maoist)	Maha Laxmi Shrestha	F	63	Mountain/ Hills	Janjati	Kath-mandu
43.	Communist Party of Nepal (Maoist)	Uma Gothe (Kapali)	F	26	Mountain/ Hills	Janjati	Bhak-tapur
44.	Communist Party of Nepal (Maoist)	Gam Bahadur Shris Magar	M	30	Mountain/ Hills	Janjati	Myagdi

45.	Communist Party of Nepal (Maoist)	Lokendra Bista Magar	M	44	Mountain/ Hills	Janjati	Rukum
46.	Communist Party of Nepal (Maoist)	Purna Bahadur Rana	M	66	Mountain/ Hills	Janjati	Baglung
47.	Communist Party of Nepal (Maoist)	Ram Bahadur Thapa Magar	M	38	Mountain/ Hills	Janjati	Udaypur
48.	Communist Party of Nepal (Maoist)	Khusiram Pakhrin	M	56	Mountain/ Hills	Janjati	Gorkha
49.	Communist Party of Nepal (Maoist)	Bir Bahadur Tamang	M	28	Mountain/ Hills	Janjati	Dhading
50.	Communist Party of Nepal (Maoist)	Dr. Indrajit Rai	M	57	Mountain/ Hills	Janjati	Bhak-tapur
51.	Communist Party of Nepal (Maoist)	Sanchpal Modan	M	35	Mountain/ Hills	Janjati	Taplejung
52.	Communist Party of Nepal (Maoist)	Tul Bahadur Majhi	M	40	Madhesi	Others	Sindhuli
53.	Communist Party of Nepal (Maoist)	Gyanendra Kumal	M	28.	Madhesi	Others	Gorkha
54.	Communist Party of Nepal (Maoist)	Chun Bahadur Thami	M	51	Mountain/ Hills	Janjati	Dolakha
55.	Communist Party of Nepal (Maoist)	Birendra Juharchan	M	51	Mountain/ Hills	Janjati	Mustang
56.	Communist Party of Nepal (Maoist)	Dilip Maharjan	M	52	Mountain/ Hills	Janjati	Kath-mandu

57.	Communist Party of Nepal (Maoist)	Shramaner Ananad	M	41	Mountain/ Hills	Janjati	Kath-mandu
58.	Communist Party of Nepal (Maoist)	Santha Lal Mul	M	53	Mountain/ Hills	Janjati	Bhak-tapur
59.	Communist Party of Nepal (Maoist)	Bimala Mijar	F	54	Mountain/ Hills	Dalit	Udaypur
60.	Communist Party of Nepal (Maoist)	Rupa B K	F	57	Mountain/ Hills	Dalit	Palpa
61.	Communist Party of Nepal (Maoist)	Santoshi B K	F	41	Mountain/ Hills	Dalit	Rolpa
62.	Communist Party of Nepal (Maoist)	Parbati Rasaili	F	33	Mountain/ Hills	Dalit	Ramech-hap
63.	Communist Party of Nepal (Maoist)	Himkumari Sunar	F	46	Mountain/ Hills	Dalit	Lamjung
64.	Communist Party of Nepal (Maoist)	Pashuram Ramtel	M	36	Mountain/ Hills	Dalit	Gorkha
65.	Communist Party of Nepal (Maoist)	Hariram Sipali	M	36	Mountain/ Hills	Dalit	Kailali
66.	Communist Party of Nepal (Maoist)	Padma Lal Bishwo-karma	M	57	Mountain/ Hills	Dalit	Ilam
67.	Communist Party of Nepal (Maoist)	Mangal B K	M	47	Mountain/ Hills	Dalit	Surkhet
68.	Communist Party of Nepal (Maoist)	Binod Pahadi	M	36	Mountain/ Hills	Dalit	Palpa

69.	Communist Party of Nepal (Maoist)	Satya Pahadi	F	30	Backward Region	Others	Dolpa
70.	Communist Party of Nepal (Maoist)	Dhirendra Upadhyaya	F	28	Backward Region	Others	Kalikot
71.	Communist Party of Nepal (Maoist)	Chhimi Lama	M	28	Backward Region	Janjati	Humla
72.	Communist Party of Nepal (Maoist)	Dharma Raj B K	M	30	Backward Region	Dalit	Bajhang
73.	Communist Party of Nepal (Maoist)	Renu Dahal	F	31	Mountain/ Hills	Others	Chitwan
74.	Communist Party of Nepal (Maoist)	Yashoda Gurung Subedi	F	39	Mountain/ Hills	Others	Manang
75.	Communist Party of Nepal (Maoist)	Khuma Subedi	F	35	Mountain/ Hills	Others	Rolpa
76.	Communist Party of Nepal (Maoist)	Gita Thagunna	F	25	Mountain/ Hills	Others	Darchula
77.	Communist Party of Nepal (Maoist)	Renuka Chaulagain	F	29	Mountain/ Hills	Others	Kavrepal-anchok
78.	Communist Party of Nepal (Maoist)	Ganga Parajuli	F	32	Mountain/ Hills	Others	Lalitpur
79.	Communist Party of Nepal (Maoist)	Shanta Neupane	F	50	Mountain/ Hills	Others	Chitwan
80.	Communist Party of Nepal (Maoist)	Uma Karki Bista	F	28	Mountain/ Hills	Others	Sankhu-wasabha

81.	Communist Party of Nepal (Maoist)	Puja Khanal	F	32	Mountain/ Hills	Others	Sunsari
82.	Communist Party of Nepal (Maoist)	Bimala K C	F	29	Mountain/ Hills	Others	Rukum
83.	Communist Party of Nepal (Maoist)	Sharada Ghimire	F	29	Mountain/ Hills	Others	Rupan-dehi
84.	Communist Party of Nepal (Maoist)	Kalpana Devi Subedi	F	48	Mountain/ Hills	Others	Sindhuli
85.	Communist Party of Nepal (Maoist)	Bharat Kumari Regmi Sharma	F	33	Mountain/ Hills	Others	Dailekh
86.	Communist Party of Nepal (Maoist)	Goma Pathak	F	25	Mountain/ Hills	Others	Syangja
87.	Communist Party of Nepal (Maoist)	Mohan Baidhya	M	61	Mountain/ Hills	Others	Dang
88.	Communist Party of Nepal (Maoist)	Nanda Kumar Prasai	M	62	Mountain/ Hills	Others	Morang
89.	Communist Party of Nepal (Maoist)	Narayan Prasad Poudel	M	51	Mountain/ Hills	Others	Dang
90.	Communist Party of Nepal (Maoist)	Mohamad safik Miya	M	34	Mountain/ Hills	Others	Syangja
91.	Communist Party of Nepal (Maoist)	Sriram Dhakal	M	51	Mountain/ Hills	Others	Tanahu
92.	Communist Party of Nepal (Maoist)	Ishwari Prasad Dahal	M	66	Mountain/ Hills	Others	Kath-mandu

93.	Communist Party of Nepal (Maoist)	Ashok Kumar Rokaya Chhetri	M	45	Mountain/ Hills	Others	Banke
94.	Communist Party of Nepal (Maoist)	Maya Prasad Sharma	M	44	Mountain/ Hills	Others	Jajarkot
95.	Communist Party of Nepal (Maoist)	Dinanath Sharma	M	58	Mountain/ Hills	Others	Baglung
96.	Communist Party of Nepal (Maoist)	Surya Bahadur Sen Oli	M	63	Mountain/ Hills	Others	Gulmi
97.	Communist Party of Nepal (Maoist)	Jokha Bhadur Mahara	M	44	Mountain/ Hills	Others	Rolpa
98.	Communist Party of Nepal (Maoist)	Keshav Prasad Nepal	M	48	Mountain/ Hills	Others	Sindhu-palchok
99.	Communist Party of Nepal (Maoist)	Ekraj Bhandari	M	48	Mountain/ Hills	Others	Salyan
100.	Communist Party of Nepal (Maoist)	Khim Lal Devkota	M	42	Mountain/ Hills	Others	Kaski
101.	Nepali Congress	Girija Prasad Koirala	M	84	Mountain/ Hills	Others	Morang
102.	Nepali Congress	Bal Dev Sharma Majagaiya	M	58	Mountain/ Hills	Others	Dang
103.	Nepali Congress	Laxman Prasad Ghimire	M	64	Mountain/ Hills	Others	Ramechhap
104.	Nepali Congress	Pradip Giri	M	58	Mountain/ Hills	Others	Siraha

105.	Nepali Congress	Purna Bahadur Khadka	M	52	Mountain/ Hills	Others	Surkhet
106.	Nepali Congress	Minendra Prasad Rijal	M	50	Mountain/ Hills	Others	Morang
107.	Nepali Congress	Prakash Sharan Mahat	M	47	Mountain/ Hills	Others	Nuwakot
108.	Nepali Congress	Jip Chirring Lama Sherpa	M	52	Mountain/ Hills	Janjati	Dolakha
109.	Nepali Congress	Shiva Chandra Mishra	M	63	Madhesi	Others	Saptari
110.	Nepali Congress	Indra Bahadur Gurung	M	66	Mountain/ Hills	Janjati	Syangja
111.	Nepali Congress	Ramesh Lekhak	M	43	Mountain/ Hills	Others	Kanchan- pur
112.	Nepali Congress	Puurshottam Basnet	M	63	Mountain/ Hills	Others	So- lukhum- bu
113.	Nepali Congress	Shovakar Parajuli	M	49	Mountain/ Hills	Others	Bara
114.	Nepali Congress	Jivan Prem Shrestha	M	56	Mountain/ Hills	Janjati	Gorkha
115.	Nepali Congress	Tika Ram Subba Lepcha	M	54	Mountain/ Hills	Janjati	Ilam
116.	Nepali Congress	Amrit Lal Rajbhansi	M	41	Madhesi	Janjati	Jhapa
117.	Nepali Congress	Bodhnarayan Sardar	M	51	Madhesi	Janjati	Sunsari

118.	Nepali Congress	Kumar Rai	M	59	Mountain/ Hills	Janjati	Bhojpur
119.	Nepali Congress	Pasang Sherpa	M	45	Mountain/ Hills	Janjati	Sankhu-wasabha
120.	Nepali Congress	Gokarna Rai	M	49	Mountain/ Hills	Janjati	So-lukhum-bu
121.	Nepali Congress	Ram Saroj Yadav	M	54	Madhesi	Others	Dhanusha
122.	Nepali Congress	Mahendra Yadav	M	44	Madhesi	Others	Dhanusha
123.	Nepali Congress	Jagdishwor Narsingh K C	M	41	Mountain/ Hills	Others	Nuwakot
124.	Nepali Congress	Gagan Thapa	M	31	Mountain/ Hills	Others	Kath-mandu
125.	Nepali Congress	Tirtha Ram Dangol	M	56	Mountain/ Hills	Janjati	Kath-mandu
126.	Nepali Congress	Diwakar Golcha	M	55	Madhesi	Others	Kath-mandu
127.	Nepali Congress	Ram Krishna Chitrakar	M	37	Mountain/ Hills	Janjati	Lalitpur
128.	Nepali Congress	Harshajit Lama	M	55	Mountain/ Hills	Janjati	Kavrepal-anchok
129.	Nepali Congress	Shambhu Hajara Paswan	M	41	Madhesi	Dalit	Parsa

130.	Nepali Congress	Rameshwor Prasad Rauniyar	M	41	Madhesi	Others	Parsa
131.	Nepali Congress	Dhanraj Gurung	M	42	Mountain/ Hills	Janjati	Syangja
132.	Nepali Congress	Khadga Bahadur Basyal	M	58	Mountain/ Hills	Dalit	Surkhet
133.	Nepali Congress	Badshah Kurmi	M	49	Madhesi	Others	Banke
134.	Nepali Congress	Om Prakash Sharma	M	40	Madhesi	Others	Parsa
135.	Nepali Congress	Maha Nepali	M	38	Backward Region	Dalit	Bajura
136.	Nepali Congress	Man Bahadur Mahato	M	58	Madhesi	Janjati	Kailali
137.	Nepali Congress	Chandri Ram Tamata	M	62	Mountain/ Hills	Dalit	Baitadi
138.	Nepali Congress	Uma Adhikari	F	53	Mountain/ Hills	Others	Chitwan
139.	Nepali Congress	Mina Pandey	F	55	Mountain/ Hills	Others	Sarlahi
140.	Nepali Congress	Maha Laxmi Aryal Upadhyaya	F	42	Mountain/ Hills	Others	Makwan-pur
141.	Nepali Congress	Ambika Basnet	F	58	Mountain/ Hills	Others	Kath-mandu
142.	Nepali Congress	Arju Rana Deuba	F	45	Mountain/ Hills	Others	Dadeld-hura

143.	Nepali Congress	Nirmala Prasai	F	59	Mountain/ Hills	Others	Ilam
144.	Nepali Congress	Usha Gurung	F	38	Mountain/ Hills	Janjati	Jhapa
145.	Nepali Congress	Bhutini Devi Khawas	F	40	Madhesi	Janjati	Morang
146.	Nepali Congress	Kavita Sardar Bantar	F	43	Madhesi	Dalit	Morang
147.	Nepali Congress	Ramwati Chaudhary	F	57	Madhesi	Janjati	Sunsari
148.	Nepali Congress	Lila Subba	F	55	Mountain/ Hills	Janjati	Dhankuta
149.	Nepali Congress	Sita Gurung	F	32	Mountain/ Hills	Janjati	Teh-rathum
150.	Nepali Congress	Bina Poudel	F	48	Mountain/ Hills	Others	Kath-mandu
151.	Nepali Congress	Hira Gurung	F	39	Mountain/ Hills	Janjati	Khotang
152.	Nepali Congress	Pramila Rai	F	44	Mountain/ Hills	Janjati	Udaypur
153.	Nepali Congress	Laxmi Pariyar	F	30	Mountain/ Hills	Dalit	Udaypur
154.	Nepali Congress	Munni Kumari Gupta	F	29	Madhesi	Others	Saptari
155.	Nepali Congress	Sarswati Chaudhary	F	48	Madhesi	Janjati	Dhanusha
156.	Nepali Congress	Krishna Thakur	F	54	Madhesi	Others	Dhanusha
157.	Nepali Congress	Minaxi Jha	F	42	Madhesi	Others	Dhanusha

158.	Nepali Congress	Kiran Yadav	F	40	Madhesi	Others	Mahottari
159.	Nepali Congress	Kalyani Rijal	F	46	Mountain/ Hills	Others	Kath- mandu
160.	Nepali Congress	Rama Guragain	F	43	Mountain/ Hills	Others	Kath- mandu
161.	Nepali Congress	Krishna Amatya	F	42	Mountain/ Hills	Janjati	Kath- mandu
162.	Nepali Congress	Kamala Thapa	F	49	Mountain/ Hills	Others	Kavrepal- anchok
163.	Nepali Congress	Lalit Kingring Magar	F	46	Mountain/ Hills	Janjati	Kavrepal- anchok
164.	Nepali Congress	Sun Devi Joshi	F	57	Mountain/ Hills	Janjati	Chitwan
165.	Nepali Congress	Krishna Kumari Pariyar	F	41	Mountain/ Hills	Dalit	Kaski
166.	Nepali Congress	Parvati Rana Magar (Urmila)	F	42	Mountain/ Hills	Janjati	Tanahu
167.	Nepali Congress	Savitri Singh	F	43	Madhesi	Others	Rupan- dehi
168.	Nepali Congress	Ratna Sherchan	F	51	Mountain/ Hills	Janjati	Baglung
169.	Nepali Congress	Bimala Nepali	F	29	Mountain/ Hills	Dalit	Dang

170.	Nepali Congress	Dudh Kumari Hamal	F	45	Backward Region	Others	Dolpa
171.	Nepali Congress	Mohamadi Sidiqi	F	49	Madhesi	Others	Banke
172.	Nepali Congress	Kalpana Damai	F	35	Mountain/ Hills	Dalit	Doti
173.	Nepali Congress	Ishwari Neupane	F	48	Mountain/ Hills	Others	Kailali
174.	Communist Party of Nepal (U.M.L.)	Chabbi Lal Bishwo-karma	M	45	Mountain/ Hills	Dalit	Rupan-dehi
175.	Communist Party of Nepal (U.M.L.)	Bhim Bahadur Rawal	M	52	Mountain/ Hills	Others	Achham
176.	Communist Party of Nepal (U.M.L.)	Yuvraj Karki	M	54	Mountain/ Hills	Others	Jhapa
177.	Communist Party of Nepal (U.M.L.)	Rana Dhoj Limbu	M	49	Mountain/ Hills	Janjati	Teh-rathum
178.	Communist Party of Nepal (U.M.L.)	Radha Gyawali	F	53	Mountain/ Hills	Others	Rupan-dehi
179.	Communist Party of Nepal (U.M.L.)	Lal Babu Pandit	M	49	Madhesi	Others	Morang
180.	Communist Party of Nepal (U.M.L.)	Bishnu Prasad Rimal	M	46	Mountain/ Hills	Others	Nuwakot
181.	Communist Party of Nepal (U.M.L.)	Surendra Pandey	M	49	Mountain/ Hills	Others	Dhading

182.	Communist Party of Nepal (U.M.L.)	Shankar Pokhrel	M	52	Mountain/ Hills	Others	Dang
183.	Communist Party of Nepal (U.M.L.)	Agni Prasad Kharel	M	47	Mountain/ Hills	Others	Jhapa
184.	Communist Party of Nepal (U.M.L.)	Abdul Kalam Ajaad	M	52	Madhesi	Others	Rautahat
185.	Communist Party of Nepal (U.M.L.)	Bishnu Maya Bishwo-karma	F	34	Mountain/ Hills	Dalit	Tanahu
186.	Communist Party of Nepal (U.M.L.)	Biva Kumari Karki	F	40	Mountain/ Hills	Others	Bara
187.	Communist Party of Nepal (U.M.L.)	Bina Gyawali	F	48	Mountain/ Hills	Others	Bardiya
188.	Communist Party of Nepal (U.M.L.)	Binod Kumar Chaud-hary	M	53	Madhesi	Others	Kath-mandu
189.	Communist Party of Nepal (U.M.L.)	Binda Pandey	F	41	Mountain/ Hills	Others	Nuwakot
190.	Communist Party of Nepal (U.M.L.)	Bhaire Kami	M	47	Mountain/ Hills	Dalit	Achham
191.	Communist Party of Nepal (U.M.L.)	Chiranjivi Ram Tharu	M	52	Madhesi	Janjati	Bardiya
192.	Communist Party of Nepal (U.M.L.)	Durga Pariyar	F	39	Mountain/ Hills	Dalit	Udaypur

193.	Communist Party of Nepal (U.M.L.)	Dolma Tamang	F	35	Mountain/ Hills	Janjati	Sindhu-palchok
194.	Communist Party of Nepal (U.M.L.)	Dhirendra Bahadur Shrestha	M	43	Mountain/ Hills	Janjati	Salyan
195.	Communist Party of Nepal (U.M.L.)	Devi Lal Thapa	M	45	Mountain/ Hills	Others	Jumla
196.	Communist Party of Nepal (U.M.L.)	Dal Bahadur Sunar	M	46	Mountain/ Hills	Dalit	Banke
197.	Communist Party of Nepal (U.M.L.)	Durga Likha	M	39	Mountain/ Hills	Janjati	Dhankuta
198.	Communist Party of Nepal (U.M.L.)	Dil Bahadur Karki	M	45	Mountain/ Hills	Others	Syangja
199.	Communist Party of Nepal (U.M.L.)	Govinda Ram Praja	M	33	Mountain/ Hills	Janjati	Makwan-pur
200.	Communist Party of Nepal (U.M.L.)	Govinda Nepali	M	45	Mountain/ Hills	Dalit	Nuwakot
201.	Communist Party of Nepal (U.M.L.)	Gopal Singh Bohara	M	65	Mountain/ Hills	Janjati	Darchula
202.	Communist Party of Nepal (U.M.L.)	Gopal Thakur	M	46	Madhesi	Others	Bara
203.	Communist Party of Nepal (U.M.L.)	Hasina Miya	F	57	Madhesi	Others	Syangja
204.	Communist Party of Nepal (U.M.L.)	Jaya Ghimire	F	49	Mountain/ Hills	Others	Dhanusha

205.	Communist Party of Nepal (U.M.L.)	Jali Kumari Mahato	F	27	Madhesi	Others	Siraha
206.	Communist Party of Nepal (U.M.L.)	Kiran Kumari Ray	F	40	Madhesi	Others	Sarlahi
207.	Communist Party of Nepal (U.M.L.)	Lyarakyal Lama	M	44	Mountain/ Hills	Janjati	Sindhu-palchok
208.	Communist Party of Nepal (U.M.L.)	Mansingh Rajbhansi	M	34	Madhesi	Janjati	Jhapa
209.	Communist Party of Nepal (U.M.L.)	Dr. Mangal Siddhi Manandhar	M	64	Mountain/ Hills	Janjati	Kath-mandu
210.	Communist Party of Nepal (U.M.L.)	Netra Prasad Panthi	M	54	Mountain/ Hills	Others	Rupan-dehi
211.	Communist Party of Nepal (U.M.L.)	Narayani Devi Ghimire Aryal	F	41	Mountain/ Hills	Others	Palpa
212.	Communist Party of Nepal (U.M.L.)	Naradmuni Rana	M	35	Madhesi	Janjati	Kailali
213.	Communist Party of Nepal (U.M.L.)	Najir Miya	M	56	Madhesi	Others	Ar-ghakhan-chi
214.	Communist Party of Nepal (U.M.L.)	Padma Kumari Aryal	F	40	Mountain/ Hills	Others	Syangja
215.	Communist Party of Nepal (U.M.L.)	Puran Singh Dayal	M	49	Mountain/ Hills	Dalit	Baitadi

216.	Communist Party of Nepal (U.M.L.)	Ramrati Ram	F	41	Madhesi	Dalit	Siraha
217.	Communist Party of Nepal (U.M.L.)	Ram Chandra Pyasi Kusawaha	M	44	Madhesi	Others	Bara
218.	Communist Party of Nepal (U.M.L.)	Ratna Devi Gurung	F	44	Mountain/ Hills	Janjati	Nuwakot
219.	Communist Party of Nepal (U.M.L.)	Roshan Gaha Thapa	M	44	Mountain/ Hills	Janjati	Nawal-parasi
220.	Communist Party of Nepal (U.M.L.)	Rima Kumari Nepali	F	40	Mountain/ Hills	Dalit	Rolpa
221.	Communist Party of Nepal (U.M.L.)	Ram Preet Paswan	M	54	Madhesi	Others	Saptari
222.	Communist Party of Nepal (U.M.L.)	Raj Kumar Rai	M	46	Mountain/ Hills	Janjati	Dhankuta
223.	Communist Party of Nepal (U.M.L.)	Sakuntala Lepcha	F	30	Mountain/ Hills	Janjati	Ilam
224.	Communist Party of Nepal (U.M.L.)	Lucky Sherpa	F	33	Mountain/ Hills	Janjati	Kath-mandu
225.	Communist Party of Nepal (U.M.L.)	Sita Kumari Paudel	F	50	Mountain/ Hills	Others	Chitwan
226.	Communist Party of Nepal (U.M.L.)	Savitri Bhusal	F	50	Mountain/ Hills	Others	Ar-ghakhan-chi

227.	Communist Party of Nepal (U.M.L.)	Sonam Chhejung Lama	F	52	Mountain/ Hills	Janjati	Mugu
228.	Communist Party of Nepal (U.M.L.)	Sarla Yadav	F	42	Madhesi	Others	Rautahat
229.	Communist Party of Nepal (U.M.L.)	Sharada Jha	F	41	Madhesi	Others	Dhanusha
230.	Communist Party of Nepal (U.M.L.)	Sharada Devi Kumal	F	41	Madhesi	Janjati	Chitwan
231.	Communist Party of Nepal (U.M.L.)	Shanti Maya Tamang	F	29	Mountain/ Hills	Janjati	Dolakha
232.	Communist Party of Nepal (U.M.L.)	Shanti Devi Chamar	F	34	Madhesi	Others	Nawal-parasi
233.	Communist Party of Nepal (U.M.L.)	Shanti Jirel	F	34	Mountain/ Hills	Janjati	Dolakha
234.	Communist Party of Nepal (U.M.L.)	Sapana Pradhan	F	43	Mountain/ Hills	Janjati	Kath-mandu
235.	Communist Party of Nepal (U.M.L.)	Shanii Basnet Adhikari	F	47	Mountain/ Hills	Others	Kath-mandu
236.	Communist Party of Nepal (U.M.L.)	Shanta Chaudhary	F	28	Madhesi	Others	Dang
237.	Communist Party of Nepal (U.M.L.)	Thammaya Thapa Magar	F	50	Mountain/ Hills	Janjati	Myagdi
238.	Communist Party of Nepal (U.M.L.)	Tashi Syangbo Gu-rungseni	F	42	Mountain/ Hills	Janjati	Mustang

239.	Communist Party of Nepal (U.M.L.)	Usha Kala Rai	F	38	Mountain/ Hills	Janjati	Khotang
240.	Communist Party of Nepal (U.M.L.)	Urmila Devi Shah	F	39	Madhesi	Others	Dhanusha
241.	Communist Party of Nepal (U.M.L.)	Dr. Bijaya Kumar Poudel	M	43	Mountain/ Hills	Others	Kath-mandu
242.	Communist Party of Nepal (U.M.L.)	Yashoda Devi Adhikari	F	47	Mountain/ Hills	Others	Morang
243.	Communist Party of Nepal. (U.M.L.)	Yogi Lal Yadav	M	53	Madhesi	Others	Morang
244.	Madhesi People's Rights Forum, Nepal	Ramjanam Chaudhary	M	47	Madhesi	Janjati	Kailali
245.	Madhesi People's Rights Forum	Nandan Kumar Dutta	M	49	Madhesi	Others	Saptari
246.	Madhesi People's Rights Forum	Atmaram Prasad Shah	M	48	Madhesi	Others	Bara
247.	Madhesi People's Rights Forum	Tilak Bahadur Rawal	M	58	Mountain/ Hills	Others	Kath-mandu
248.	Madhesi People's Rights Forum	Shrawan Kumar Agrawal	M	60	Madhesi	Others	Lalitpur
249.	Madhesi People's Rights Forum	Madhusudan Agrawal	M	43	Madhesi	Others	Kath-mandu
250.	Madhesi People's Rights Forum	Ram Sahaya Prasad Yadav	M	47	Madhesi	Others	Bara

251.	Madhesi People's Rights Forum	Chandrika Prasad Yadav	M	46	Madhesi	Others	Rupan-dehi
252.	Madhesi People's Rights Forum	Bishwonath Prasad Yadav	M	34	Madhesi	Others	Saptari
253.	Madhesi People's Rights Forum	Ramchandra Ray Amat	M	52	Madhesi	Others	Sunsari
254.	Madhesi People's Rights Forum	Shiv Narayan Urav	M	49	Madhesi	Janjati	Sunsari
255.	Madhesi People's Rights Forum	Srimati Sandhya Devi	F	42	Madhesi	Others	Banke
256.	Madhesi People's Rights Forum	Nilam Verma	F	48	Madhesi	Others	Rautahat
257.	Madhesi People's Rights Forum	Lalita Shah	F	29	Madhesi	Others	Sunsari
258.	Madhesi People's Rights Forum	Kalawati Devi Dusad	F	46	Madhesi	Dalit	Bara
259.	Madhesi People's Rights Forum	Rambha Devi	F	50	Madhesi	Others	Rautahat
260.	Madhesi People's Rights Forum	Surita Kumari Shah	F	42	Madhesi	Janjati	Dhanusha
261.	Madhesi People's Rights Forum	Aasha Kumari Sardar	F	30	Madhesi	Dalit	Morang
262.	Madhesi People's Rights Forum	Salma Khatoon Mi-krani	F	37	Madhesi	Others	Sarlahi

263.	Madhesi People's Rights Forum	Durga Devi Mahato	F	32	Madhesi	Janjati	Parsa
264.	Madhesi People's Rights Forum	Sewaki Devi Das Tatma	F	36	Madhesi	Dalit	Siraha
265.	Madhesi People's Rights Forum	Savita Devi Yadav	F	33	Madhesi	Others	Sunsari
266.	Tarai Madhes Loktantrik Party	Mahendra Prasad Yadav	M	70	Madhesi	Others	Sarlahi
267.	Tarai Madhes Loktantrik Party	Kashi Devi Jha	F	62	Madhesi	Others	Dhanusha
268.	Tarai Madhes Loktantrik Party	Arvindra Shah	M	47	Madhesi	Others	Dhanusha
269.	Tarai Madhes Loktantrik Party	Kavindra Nath Thakur	M	56	Madhesi	Others	Dhanusha
270.	Tarai Madhes Loktantrik Party	Urmila Mahto Koiri	F	44	Madhesi	Others	Sarlahi
271.	Tarai Madhes Loktantrik Party	Chandan Shah	F	33	Madhesi	Others	Rautahat
272.	Tarai Madhes Loktantrik Party	Basnti Jha	F	52	Madhesi	Others	Mahottari
273.	Tarai Madhes Loktantrik Party	Bimal Kumar Kedia	M	46	Madhesi	Others	Rautahat
274.	Tarai Madhes Loktantrik Party	Jay Prakash Yadav	M	48	Madhesi	Others	Bara

275.	Tarai Madhes Loktantrik Party	Ramani Ram	F	40	Mountain/ Hills	Dalit	Saptari
276.	Tarai Madhes Loktantrik Party	Salahudin Musalman	M	46	Madhesi	Others	Kapil-vastu
277.	Rastriya Prajatantra Party	Lokendra Bahadur Chand	M	66	Mountain/ Hills	Others	Baitadi
278.	Rastriya Prajatantra Party	Pritibha Rana	F	60	Mountain/ Hills	Others	Bardiya
279.	Rastriya Prajatantra Party	Surya Bahadur K C	M	51	Mountain/ Hills	Others	Kaski
280.	Rastriya Prajatantra Party	Allaudin Ansari	M	55	Madhesi	Others	Nawal-parasi
281.	Rastriya Prajatantra Party	Dal Kumari Sunwar	F	65	Mountain/ Hills	Janjati	Ramech-hap
282.	Rastriya Prajatantra Party	Navodita Chaudhary	F	30	Madhesi	Janjati	Sunsari
283.	Rastriya Prajatantra Party	Babita Devi Dhobi	F	34	Madhesi	Dalit	Rupan-dehi
284.	Rastriya Prajatantra Party	Chalan Bahadur Ta-mang	M	52	Mountain/ Hills	Janjati	Sindhu-palchok
285.	Communist Party of Nepal (ML)	Chandra Prakash Mainali	M	56	Mountain/ Hills	Others	Jhapa
286.	Communist Party of Nepal (ML)	Nilam K C (Khadka)	F	44	Mountain/ Hills	Others	Jhapa

287.	Communist Party of Nepal (ML)	Janak Kumari Chalise	F	47	Mountain/ Hills	Others	Lalitpur
288.	Communist Party of Nepal (ML)	Tilak Bahadur Thapa Magar	M	37	Mountain/ Hills	Janjati	Sarlahi
289.	Communist Party of Nepal (ML)	Sharada Nepali	F	42	Mountain/ Hills	Dalit	Bardiya
290.	Communist Party of Nepal (ML)	Yadubansa Jha Mai-thali Bahun	M	50	Madhesi	Others	Dhanusha
291.	Communist Party of Nepal (ML)	Parvati Mahato (Kumal)	F	29	Madhesi	Janjati	Chitwan
292.	Communist Party of Nepal (ML)	Damodar Chaudhary	M	64	Madhesi	Janjati	Dang
293.	Janamorcha Nepal	Durga Jayanti Rai	F	32	Mountain/ Hills	Janjati	Khotang
294.	Janamorcha Nepal	Ram Kumar Yadav	M	58	Madhesi	Others	Siraha
295.	Janamorcha Nepal	Bhim Prasad Gautam	M	58	Mountain/ Hills	Others	Tanahu
296.	Janamorcha Nepal	Sita Pokhrel	F	32	Mountain/ Hills	Others	Tanahu
297.	Janamorcha Nepal	Bishwo Bhakta Dulal	M	40	Mountain/ Hills	Dalit	Kath-mandu
298.	Communist Party of Nepal (United)	Chandra Dev Joshi	M	66	Mountain/ Hills	Others	Kath-mandu

299.	Communist Party of Nepal (United)	Kalpana Rana	F	48	Mountain/ Hills	Others	Kath- mandu
300.	Communist Party of Nepal (United)	Sunil Babu Pant	M	36	Mountain/ Hills	Others	Gorkha
301.	Communist Party of Nepal (United)	Ramshila Thakur	F	30	Madhesi	Others	Mahottari
302.	Communist Party of Nepal (United)	Radhavbir Joshi	M	45	Mountain/ Hills	Janjati	Kath- mandu
303.	Sadhvawana Party	Gauri Mahto Koiri	F	48	Madhesi	Others	Sunsari
304.	Sadhvawana Party	Ram Naresh Ray	M	48	Madhesi	Others	Sarlahi
305.	Sadhvawana Party	Anil Kumar Jha	M	41	Madhesi	Others	Rautahat
306.	Sadhvawana Party	Laxman Lal Karna	M	61	Madhesi	Others	Parsa
307.	Sadhvawana Party	Malamati Devi Rana	F	47	Mountain/ Hills	Janjati	Kailali
308.	Rastriya Prajatantra Party Nepal	Chandra Bahadur Gurung	M	53	Mountain/ Hills	Janjati	Syangja
309.	Rastriya Prajatantra Party Nepal	Ramnarayan Singh	M	69	Madhesi	Others	Sarlahi
310.	Rastriya Prajatantra Party Nepal	Kunti Shah	F	30	Mountain/ Hills	Others	Dailekh
311.	Rastriya Prajatantra Party Nepal	Babina Moktan Ta- mang	F	34	Mountain/ Hills	Janjati	Jhapa
312.	Rastriya Janshakti Party	Prakash Chandra Lohani	M	64	Mountain/ Hills	Others	Nuwakot

313.	Rastriya Janshakti Party	Arjun Rai	M	46	Mountain/ Hills	Janjati	Khotang
314.	Rastriya Janshakti Party	Phulmati Devi Chaud-hary	F	46	Mountain/ Hills	Janjati	Kailali
315.	Rastriya Janamorcha	Santa Bahadur Nepali	M	52	Mountain/ Hills	Dalit	Ar-ghakhan-chi
316.	Rastriya Janamorcha	Mina Pun	F	35	Mountain/ Hills	Janjati	Baglung
317.	Rastriya Janamorcha	Rashmiraj Nepali	M	65	Mountain/ Hills	Others	Dang
318.	Nepal Workers and Peasants Party	Navraj Koirala	M	43	Backward Region	Others	Kalikot
319.	Nepal Workers and Peasants Party	Lila Nyaichaai	F	27	Mountain/ Hills	Janjati	Bhak-tapur
320.	Rastriya Janmukti Party	Malawar Singh Thapa	M	63	Mountain/ Hills	Janjati	Syangja
321.	Rastriya Janmukti Party	Chhiyama Rai	F	64	Mountain/ Hills	Janjati	Sunsari
322.	Communist Party of Nepal (Unified)	Pari Thapa	M	46	Mountain/ Hills	Janjati	Baglung
323.	Communist Party of Nepal (Unified)	Radha Devi Timalsena	F	47	Mountain/ Hills	Others	Kath-mandu

324.	Nepal Sadvawana Party (Anandidevi)	Sarita Giri	F	46	Madhesi	Others	Siraha
325.	Nepal Sadvawana Party (Anandidevi)	Motilal Dugad	M	47	Madhesi	Others	Morang
326.	Nepali Janta Dal	Dr. Bishwonath Prasad Agrawal	M	65	Madhesi	Others	Lalitpur
327.	Nepali Janta Dal	Gayatri Shah	F	26	Madhesi	Others	Sarlahi
328.	Federal Democratic National Forum	Raj Kumar Limbu (Nalbo)	M	27	Mountain/ Hills	Janjati	Morang
329.	Federal Democratic National Forum	Rukmini Chaudhary	F	30	Mountain/ Hills	Janjati	Dang
330.	Samajwadi Prajatantrik Janta Party, Nepal	Prem Bahadur Singh	M	54	Backward Region	Others	Kalikot
331.	Dalit Janjati Party	Bishwendra Paswan	M	47	Madhesi	Dalit	Siraha
332.	Nepal Pariwal Dal	Eknath Dhakal	M	34	Mountain/ Hills	Others	Gorkha
333.	Nepal Rastriya Party	Buddha Ratna Manandhar	M	63	Mountain/ Hills	Janjati	Kath- mandu
334.	Nepal Loktantrik Samajbadi Dal	Laxmi Lal Chaudhary	M	64	Mountain/ Hills	Janjati	Saptari
335.	Chure Bhawar Rastriya Ekata Party, Nepal	Keshav Prasad Mainali	M	55	Mountain/ Hills	Others	Sarlahi

APPENDIX – X

Constituent Assembly Election Regional Trends

		Ecological Belt			Nepal	Development Regions				
		Mountain	Hill	Tarai	Nepal	Eastern	Central	Western	Mid-Western	Far-Western
Turnout	First Past the Post	60.8 %	58.9 %	64.5 %	61.7 %	60.4 %	64.5 %	58.7 %	64.6 %	57.9 %
	Proportional Representation	62.9 %	60.6 %	65.8 %	63.3 %	61.8 %	66.1 %	60.2 %	66.6 %	59.8 %
Invalid	First Past the Post	4.1 %	4.3 %	6.0 %	5.2 %	6.1 %	5.6 %	4.4 %	3.9 %	4.6 %
	Proportional Representation	3.3 %	3.2 %	4.1 %	3.7 %	4.3 %	3.7 %	3.3 %	3.1 %	3.7 %
Margin	FPTP 1st place – 2nd place	18.7 %	15.5 %	10.7 %	14.8 %	10.1 %	13.4 %	11.7 %	26.0 %	13.6 %

APPENDIX – XI

Voting Percentage under FPTP

	Party / Total %	100.0 %	100.0 %	100.0 %	100.0 %	100.0 %	100.0 %	100.0 %	100.0 %	100.0 %
FPTP Percent of Seats	Communist Party of Nepal (Maoist)	72.7 %	60.8 %	36.2 %	50.0 %	41.1 %	45.7 %	36.7 %	81.8 %	71.4 %
	Nepali Congress	9.1 %	18.6 %	13.8 %	15.4 %	12.5 %	19.8 %	20.4 %	3.0 %	14.3 %
	Communist Party of Nepal (UML)	18.2 %	17.6 %	9.5 %	13.8 %	14.3 %	9.9 %	22.4 %	9.1 %	14.3 %
	Madhesi People's Rights Forum, Nepal	0.0 %	0.0 %	25.9 %	12.5 %	28.6%	8.6 %	10.2 %	6.1 %	0.0 %
	Janamorcha Nepal	0.0 %	0.0 %	1.7 %	0.8 %	0.0 %	2.5 %	0.0 %	0.0 %	0.0 %
	Nepal Workers and Peasants Party	0.0 %	2.0 %	0.0 %	0.8 %	0.0 %	2.5 %	0.0 %	0.0 %	0.0 %
	Rastriya Janamorcha	0.0 %	1.0 %	0.0 %	0.4 %	0.0 %	0.0 %	2.0 %	0.0 %	0.0 %
	Sadhvawana party	0.0 %	0.0 %	3.4 %	1.7 %	1.8 %	3.7 %	0.0 %	0.0 %	0.0 %
	Tarai Madhes Loktantrik Party	0.0 %	0.0 %	7.8 %	3.8 %	0.0 %	6.2 %	8.2 %	0.0 %	0.0 %
	Others	0.0 %	0.0 %	1.7 %	0.8 %	1.8 %	1.2 %	0.0 %	0.0 %	0.0 %
	Total Seats	**22**	**102**	**116**	**240**	**56**	**81**	**49**	**33**	**21**

APPENDIX – XII

Voting Percentage Under PRS

PR Percent of Votes	Party / Total %	100.0 %	100.0 %	100.0 %	100.0 %	100.0 %	100.0 %	100.0 %	100.0 %	100.0 %
	Communist Party of Nepal (Maoist)	38.8 %	34.9 %	22.9 %	29.3 %	23.1 %	26.6 %	29.2 %	41.7 %	37.2 %
	Nepali Congress	21.0 %	23.7 %	18.9 %	21.1 %	20.7 %	19.3 %	24.2 %	19.9 %	24.3 %
	Communist Party of Nepal (UML)	24.3 %	23.8 %	16.7 %	20.3 %	21.5 %	19.2 %	21.8 %	18.5 %	21.1 %
	Madhesi People's Rights Forum, Nepal	0.1 %	0.1 %	12.7 %	6.3 %	11.8 %	6.8 %	4.1 %	2.8 %	0.5 %
	Janamorcha Nepal	1.1 %	1.6 %	1.5 %	1.5 %	1.6 %	2.1 %	0.9 %	0.9 %	1.6 %
	Nepal Workers and Peasants Party	1.0 %	1.2 %	0.2 %	0.7 %	0.2 %	1.3 %	0.1 %	1.2 %	0.2 %
	Rastriya Janamorcha	0.4 %	1.6 %	0.5 %	1.0 %	0.2 %	0.3 %	2.2 %	2.4 %	1.2 %
	Sadhvawana party	0.0 %	0.0 %	3.1 %	1.6 %	1.8 %	2.6 %	0.7 %	0.7 %	0.1 %
	Tárai Madhes Loktantrik Party	0.1 %	0.1 %	6.3 %	3.2 %	1.4 %	5.7 %	4.1 %	0.2 %	0.1 %
	Others	13.2 %	13.0 %	17.1 %	15.0 %	17.8 %	16.1 %	12.7 %	11.7 %	13.6 %

APPENDIX - XIII

Number of Voters in Different Elections

Total Voters	1991	%	1994	%	Change	1999	%	% change 1991	& change 1999
Total votes polled	11191777	100.0	12296219	100	+110442 0.1%	13491831	100	2300054 20.5	1195612
Invalid votes	322023	4.42	241071	3.16	1.26	384739	4.40	.38	1.24

Source : Documents of the Election Commission, HMG, Nepal

APPENDIX - XIV

Party-wise Performance in 1991 Elections

Name of the Parties	Total Candi-dates	Seats Won	% of Total Seats	Votes Received	% of votes polled
Nepali Congress	204	110	53.66	2752452	37.75
NCP (UML)	177	69	33.66	2040102	27.98
UPF	70	9	4.39	351904	4.83
NSP	75	6	2.92	298610	4.10
RPP (Chand)	154	3	1.46	478604	6.56
RPP (Thapa)	163	1	0.49	392499	5.38
NCP (Democratic)	75	2	0.98	177323	2.43
NMKP	30	2	0.98	91335	1.25
NRIM	50			34509	0.47
NCP	6			2562	0.04
JD (SP)	15			5760	0.08
AP	1			94	0.00
RIPN	9			4280	0.06
BJD	1			2012	0.03
NCP (BURMA)	35			16698	0.23

APPENDIX - XV

Popular Votes and Seats Represented in the House of Representatives

Election 1991 Election 1994 Election 1999

S. No.	Political Parties	Election 1991		Election 1994		Election 1999	
		Popular Vote in %	Seats (%)	Popular Vote in %	Seats (%)	Popular Vote in %	Seats (%)
1	NC	37.75	110 (53.65)	33.38	83 (40.49)	36.14	111 (54.15)
2	CPN (UML)	27.98	69 (33.65)	30.85	88 (42.93)	30.74	68 (34.63)
3	RPP	-----	-----	17.95	20 (9.76)	10.14	11 (5.37)
4	RPP (C)	6.56	3 (1.46)	-----	-----	3.33	0
5	RPP (T)	5.38	1 (0.48)	-----	-----	-----	-----
6	SJMN (UPF)	4.83	9 (4.39)	1.32	0	0.84	1 (0.49)
7	NSP	4.1	6 (2.92)	3.49	3 (1.46)	3.13	5 (2.44)
8	NWPP	1.25	2 (0.97)	0.98	4 (1.95)	0.55	1 (0.49)
9	RJM	-----	-----	-----	-----	1.37	5 (2.44)
10	CPN (D)	2.43	2 (0.97)	-----	-----	-----	-----
11	CPN (ML)	-----	-----	-----	0	6.38	0
12	RJMP	0.47	0	1.05	0	1.07	0

APPENDIX - XVI

Social Composition of Central Committees of Major Political Parties, 1999

S. No.	Political Parties	Social Group and Representation					Total
		Bahun-Chhetri	Janajati	Madhesi	Dalit	Newar	
1	Nepali Congress (NC)	22 (70.97)	3 (9.68)	4 (12.9)	----	2 (6.45)	31
2	Nepal Communist Party (UML)	28 (87.5)	1 (3.13)	1 (3.13)	----	2 (6.25)	32
3	Nepal Communist Party (ML)	18 (50)	5 (13.89)	4 (11.11)	----	9 (25)	36
4	Rastriya Prajatantra Party (RPP)	15 (44.12)	8 (23.53)	9 (26.47)	----	2 (5.88)	34
5	Rastriya Prajatantra Party (C)	14 (43.75)	8 (25)	7 (21.88)	----	3 (9.38)	32
Total 1999		97 (58.8)	25 (15.1)	26 (15.7)	----	18 (10.9)	165
Population Percentage 1991		31.6	22.3	30.9	8.6	5.6	
Leadership of Major Parties, 1959		50 (63.2)	11 (13.9)	7 (8.8)	----	11 (13.9)	79

APPENDIX – XVII

First Past The Post by Districts

S. No.	District	Constituencies	Communist Party of Nepal (Maoist)	Nepali Congress	Communist Party of Nepal (UML)	Madhesi People's Rights Forum, Nepal	Others	Male	Female	Registered Voters	FPTP Votes Cast	Turnout	Invalid Votes	Invalid %
1	Taplejung	2	0	1	1	0	0	2	0	107,714	56,557	52.50%	2,212	3.90%
2	Panchthar	2	0	1	1	0	0	2	0	155,983	88,354	56.60%	5,079	5.70%
3	Ilam	3	0	1	2	0	0	3	0	212,055	139,333	65.70%	5,809	4.20%
4	Jhapa	7	5	1	1	0	0	6	1	628,666	372,924	59.30%	21,665	5.80%
5	Sankhuwasabha	2	1	0	1	0	0	2	0	132,118	66,327	50.20%	3,510	5.30%
6	Terhathum	1	0	1	0	0	0	1	0	90,935	51,024	56.10%	2,194	4.30%

7	Bhojpur	2	2	0	0	0	0	2	0	166,050	81,375	49.00%	5,181	6.40%
8	Dhankuta	2	2	0	0	0	0	2	0	125,727	74,250	59.10%	3,291	4.40%
9	Morang	9	4	1	0	4	0	9	0	648,894	421,597	65.00%	24,900	5.90%
10	Sunsari	6	1	0	2	3	0	6	0	477,973	303,325	63.50%	19,318	6.40%
11	Solukhumbu	1	1	0	0	0	0	1	0	84,182	42,300	50.20%	1,899	4.50%
12	Khotang	2	2	0	0	0	0	1	1	182,794	90,102	49.30%	5,453	6.10%
13	Okhaldhunga	2	2	0	0	0	0	2	0	129,378	66,564	51.40%	3,095	4.60%
14	Udyapur	3	2	1	0	0	0	3	0	220,028	119,995	54.50%	6,450	5.40%
15	Saptari	6	0	0	0	4	2	5	1	416,712	290,035	69.60%	23,479	8.10%
16	Siraha	6	1	0	0	5	0	6	0	434,353	283,319	65.20%	21,553	7.60%
17	Dolakha	2	2	0	0	0	0	1	1	165,928	96,853	58.40%	3,376	3.50%
18	Ramechhap	2	2	0	0	0	0	2	0	180,026	97,472	54.10%	4,090	4.20%
19	Sindhuli	3	2	0	1	0	0	2	1	202,918	116,761	57.50%	5,171	4.40%
20	Dhanusa	7	1	3	2	1	0	6	1	463,225	288,528	62.30%	22,290	7.70%
21	Mahottari	6	0	0	0	3	3	6	0	394,473	249,183	63.20%	17,861	7.20%
22	Sarlahi	6	0	0	2	1	3	5	1	471,489	326,128	69.20%	19,803	6.10%
23	Rasuwa	1	1	0	0	0	0	1	0	32,442	21,434	66.10%	908	4.20%
24	Dhading	3	3	0	0	0	0	2	1	276,259	174,304	63.10%	7,514	4.30%
25	Nuwakot	3	2	1	0	0	0	2	1	247,215	146,243	59.20%	9,495	6.50%
26	Kathmandu	10	4	6	0	0	0	8	2	596,495	388,223	65.10%	14,493	3.70%

27	Bhaktapur	2	0	0	0	0	2	2	0	159,464	118,469	74.30%	3,861	3.30%
28	Lalitpur	3	3	0	0	0	0	2	1	235,328	157,897	67.10%	5,275	3.30%
29	Kabhre	4	3	0	1	0	0	4	0	321,705	210,410	65.40%	9,155	4.40%
30	Sindhupalchok	3	3	0	0	0	0	3	0	260,357	160,411	61.60%	8,458	5.30%
31	Makwanpur	4	4	0	0	0	0	3	1	288,868	173,773	60.20%	9,747	5.60%
32	Rautahat	6	2	2	0	0	2	6	0	373,650	262,408	70.20%	18,459	7.00%
33	Bara	6	2	1	0	1	2	6	0	396,003	279,823	70.70%	20,100	7.20%
34	Parsa	5	0	3	1	1	0	4	1	363,013	241,085	66.40%	17,773	7.40%
35	Chitawan	5	3	0	1	0	1	5	0	382,580	240,151	62.80%	10,532	4.40%
36	Gorkha	3	3	0	0	0	0	2	1	249,945	161,996	64.80%	5,408	3.30%
37	Manang	1	1	0	0	0	0	1	0	7,407	2,971	40.10%	63	2.10%
38	Lamjung	2	1	0	1	0	0	2	0	153,335	89,390	58.30%	2,812	3.10%
39	Kaski	4	3	0	1	0	0	3	1	315,635	177,387	56.20%	6,434	3.60%
40	Tanahu	3	1	1	1	0	0	3	0	267,618	140,293	52.40%	7,950	5.70%
41	Syangja	3	0	2	1	0	0	3	0	295,442	153,405	51.90%	6,948	4.50%
42	Gulmi	3	2	0	1	0	0	3	0	261,669	138,944	53.10%	5,688	4.10%
43	Palpa	3	1	0	2	0	0	2	1	215,281	121,816	56.60%	3,833	3.10%
44	Arghakhanchi	2	1	1	0	0	0	1	1	180,694	100,828	55.80%	3,882	3.90%
45	Nawalparasi	6	2	2	0	1	1	5	1	428,018	273,671	63.90%	14,712	5.40%
46	Rupandehi	7	1	1	2	3	0	7	0	522,898	333,198	63.70%	16,645	5.00%

47	Kapilbastu	5	0	1	0	1	3	5	0	348,954	220,505	63.20%	13,309	6.00%
48	Mustang	1	0	0	1	0	0	1	0	11,889	6,167	51.90%	175	2.80%
49	Myagdi	1	1	0	0	0	0	1	0	88,147	50,124	56.90%	1,266	2.50%
50	Baglung	3	0	1	1	0	1	3	0	226,365	131,928	58.30%	5,400	4.10%
51	Parbat	2	1	1	0	0	0	2	0	145,134	79,074	54.50%	2,423	3.10%
52	Rukum	2	2	0	0	0	0	1	1	130,947	90,668	69.20%	2,503	2.80%
53	Rolpa	2	2	0	0	0	0	1	1	153,966	88,903	57.70%	3,089	3.50%
54	Pyuthan	2	2	0	0	0	0	2	0	160,561	94,577	58.90%	3,763	4.00%
55	Salyan	2	2	0	0	0	0	2	0	159,894	98,456	61.60%	3,080	3.10%
56	Dang	5	5	0	0	0	0	3	2	358,860	217,695	60.70%	9,784	4.50%
57	Dolpa	1	1	0	0	0	0	1	0	21,932	17,522	79.90%	776	4.40%
58	Mugu	1	1	0	0	0	0	1	0	33,720	25,429	75.40%	682	2.70%
59	Jumla	1	1	0	0	0	0	1	0	61,868	43,939	71.00%	1,372	3.10%
60	Kalikot	1	1	0	0	0	0	1	0	80,252	56,671	70.60%	2,413	4.30%
61	Humla	1	1	0	0	0	0	1	0	30,089	23,987	79.70%	528	2.20%
62	Jajarkot	2	2	0	0	0	0	2	0	97,304	67,218	69.10%	2,449	3.60%
63	Dailekh	2	0	1	1	0	0	2	0	167,786	102,693	61.20%	5,423	5.30%
64	Surkhet	3	1	0	2	0	0	2	1	214,183	135,213	63.10%	4,719	3.50%
65	Banke	4	2	0	0	2	0	3	1	253,622	174,304	68.70%	8,557	4.90%
66	Bardiya	4	4	0	0	0	0	3	1	274,180	184,467	67.30%	5,617	3.00%

67	Bajura	1	0	1	0	0	0	1	0	80,721	55,089	68.20%	1,319	2.40%
68	Achham	2	1	0	1	0	0	2	0	192,856	108,972	56.50%	5,443	5.00%
69	Bajhang	2	1	0	1	0	0	2	0	129,719	74,570	57.50%	2,848	3.80%
70	Doti	2	1	0	1	0	0	2	0	145,969	73,334	50.20%	3,589	4.90%
71	Kailali	6	6	0	0	0	0	4	2	475,436	285,354	60.00%	11,557	4.10%
72	Darchula	1	1	0	0	0	0	1	0	86,661	55,951	64.60%	2,329	4.20%
73	Baitadi	2	2	0	0	0	0	1	1	171,212	91,640	53.50%	6,128	6.70%
74	Dadeldhura	1	0	1	0	0	0	1	0	100,407	54,794	54.60%	2,926	5.30%
75	Kanchanpur	4	3	1	0	0	0	4	0	284,319	166,051	58.40%	8,720	5.30%
	Total	**240**	**120**	**37**	**33**	**30**	**20**	**211**	**29**	**17,609,895**	**10,866,131**	**61.70%**	**560,011**	**5.20%**
	By-Elections	**5**	**2**	**1**	**0**	**2**	**0**	**5**	**0**					
	Final Seats	**235**	**118**	**36**	**33**	**28**	**20**	**206**	**29**					

Select Bibliography

Books

1. Acharya Bhimarajan, *Making Constitution Through Constituent Assembly*, Pairaer Prakashan, Kathmandu, 2006.
2. *Act Relating to Electoral Rolls*, Act No. 32, Kathmandu, 29 December, 2006.
3. Brown Louise T., *The Challenge to Democracy in Nepal : A Political History*, Routledge, London, 1996.
4. Baral Lok Raj (ed.), *Nepal: Facets of Maoist Insurgency*, Adroit, Delhi, 2006.
5. Baral Lok Raj (ed.), *Nepal: Quest For Participatory Democracy*, Adroit Publishers, Delhi, 2006.
6. Dahal Ram Kumar, *Constitutional and Political Developments in Nepal*, Ratna Pushtak Bhandar, Kathmandu, 2001.
7. *Election to Members of the Constituent Assembly*, Act No. 2, Kathmandu, 22 June, 2007.
8. Gellner David N., et.al. (eds), *Nationalism and Ethnicity in a Himalayan Kingdom, The Politics of Culture in Contemporary Nepal*, Harward Academic Publishers, Amsterdam, 1997.
9. Gellner David N. Hachhethu Krishna (eds), *Local Democracy in South Asia, Micro Processes of Democratization in Nepal and its Neighbours*, SAGE, New Delhi, 2008.
10. Hachhethu Krishna, *The State of Democracy in Nepal*, Survey Report, SDSAIN, Kathmandu, 2004.
11. Hutt Michael (ed.), *Himalayan People's War : Nepal's Maoist Rebellion*, Hurst & Co., London, 2005.
12. International Crisis Group, *Nepal's Election : A Peaceful Revolution* ? Asia Report No. 155, 3 July 2008.
13. International Crisis Group, *Nepal's New Political Landscape*, Asia Report No. 150, 3 July 2008.
14. Joshi Bhuwan Lal & Rose Leo E., *Democratic Innovations in Nepal : A Case of Political Acculturation*, University of California Press, California, 1966.

15. Lawati Mahendra, *Towards A Democratic Nepal : Inclusive Political Institutions For a Multicultural Society*, SAGE, New Delhi, 2005.
16. Mahat Ram Sharan, *In Defence of Democracy : Dynamics and Fault Lines of Nepal's Political Economy*, Adroit, Delhi, 2005.
17. Pyakurel Udhav P., *Maoist Movement in Nepal : A Sociological Perspective*, Adroit, Delhi, 2007.
18. Shukla Deeptima, *Monarchy in Nepal*, Kalinga, Delhi, 2000.
19. Sharma Pitamber, *Unraveling The Mosaic : Spatial Aspects of Ethnicity in Nepal*, Himal Book, Lalitpur, Nepal, 2008.
20. Upreti B.C., *Nepal Dilemmas of Development and Change in Far Western Hills*, Indus, Delhi, 2006.
21. Upreti Bishm Raj, *Armed Conflict and Peace Process in Nepal*, Adroit, Delhi, 2006.
22. Upreti B.C., *Nepal, Democracy at Cross Roads ; Post 1990 Dynamics, Issues and Challenges*, Kanishka Publishers Distributor, Delhi, 2007.
23. Upreti B.C. & Upadhyaya Shashi (ed.), *State and Democracy in South Asia*, Sumit Enterprises, Delhi, 2008.
24. Upreti B.C., *Maoist in Nepal : From Insurgency to Political Mainstream*, Kalpaz Publications, New Delhi, 2008.

Articles

1. Acharya Bhimarjan, "Technicalities of Constituent Assembly", *Readings on Government and Development* (Kathmandu) Vol. X, 2007.
2. Acharya Bhimarjan, "Constituent Assembly Pathways to Constitution Making", *Readings on Government and Development*, Vol. VII, 2006.
3. Acharya Bhimarjan, " Constitution Making and Non Negotiable Principles", *Readings on Government and Development*, Vol. VII, 2007.
4. Baral Lok Raj, "Imperative of Federalism", *The Kathmandu Post*, February 19, 2008.
5. Bhart C.D., "Role of Civil Society in Conflict Resolution, *Rising Nepal*, July 27, 2006.
6. Dhakal Amit, "Koirala Advocates Ceremonial Monarchy", *The Hindu*, June 15, 2006.
7. Josse M.R., "PLA Integration: Tough Nest to Crack", *People's Review*, June 19, 2008.

8. Kumar Dhrub, "Nepal's Future: Order in Paradox", *Aakrosh*, Vol. II, November 40, July 2008.
9. Middleton Townsend & Shneiderman Sara, "Reservations, Federalism and the Politics of Recognition in Nepal", *Economic & Political Weekly*, May 10, 2008.
10. Mikesell Stephen and CheneMary Das, "Baburan Bhattarai : For A New Nepal", *Economic and Political Weekly*, 10-16 May, 2008.
11. Mukherji Deb et.at., Debate – "Dealing With Maoist Nepal", *Indian Foreign Affairs Journal*, Vol 3, No. 3, July-September, 2008.
12. Thapa Manjushree, "India in its Nepali Backyard", *Open Democracy*, May 2, 2008.
13. Upreti B.C., "State and Society in Nepal : The Emerging Issues of Their Restructuring and Transformation", *Indian Journal of Nepalese Studies*, Vol. XIII, 2007.
14. Upreti B.C., "Civil Society and Democracy in Nepal", *Indian Journal of Nepalese Studies*, Vol. XIV, 2008.
15. Upreti B.C., "Rebuilding Democracy in Nepal : Issues and Challenges", *Readings on Government Development*, Vol. X, 2007.
16. Upreti B.C., "Challenges in the Post Election Scenario in Nepal", *Economic and Political Weeky*, Vol. XLIV, No.11, March 14, 2009.
17. Varderajan Sidharth, "In Nepal the Beginning of An End", *The Hindu*, April 22, 2006.

Index

N

P

R

S